Create a Winning Team

WITHDRAWN
from Toronto Public Library

Teach Yourself®

Create a Winning Team

A practical guide to successful teamworking

Kevin Benfield

Hodder Education

338 Euston Road, London NW1 3BH.

Hodder Education is an Hachette UK company

First published in UK 2011 by Hodder Education

First published in US 2011 by The McGraw-Hill Companies, Inc.

This edition published 2011.

British Library Cataloguing in Publication Data: a catalogue record
for this title is available from the British Library.

Library of Congress Catalog Card Number: on file.

10 9 8 7 6 5 4 3 2 1

The publisher has used its best endeavours to ensure that any
website addresses referred to in this book are correct and active at
the time of going to press. However, the publisher and the author
have no responsibility for the websites and can make no guarantee
that a site will remain live or that the content will remain relevant,
decent or appropriate.

The publisher has made every effort to mark as such all words
which it believes to be trademarks. The publisher should also
like to make it clear that the presence of a word in the book,
whether marked or unmarked, in no way affects its legal status as
a trademark.

Every reasonable effort has been made by the publisher to trace the
copyright holders of material in this book. Any errors or omissions
should be notified in writing to the publisher, who will endeavour to
rectify the situation for any reprints and future editions.

Hachette UK's policy is to use papers that are natural, renewable
and recyclable products and made from wood grown in sustainable
forests. The logging and manufacturing processes are expected to
conform to the environmental regulations of the country of origin.

www.hoddereducation.co.uk

Typeset by Cenveo Publisher Services.

Printed in Great Britain by CPI Cox & Wyman, Reading.

**Also available
in ebook**

Acknowledgements

Chapter 8 'How to develop your team' in the section on 'Do team-building activities work?' a number of companies made a valuable contribution to that topic. These are:

- Katalan: www.katalan.co.uk;
- Leadership Resources: www.leadershipresources.co.uk;
- R&A Consultancy & Training: www.raconsultancy.com;
- Sandstone: www.sandstone.co.uk;
- Symbiosis Consulting: www.symbiosisconsulting.co.uk.

The individuals quoted are referenced in context.

Thank you to these companies for their contribution which is gratefully acknowledged.

Contents

Meet the author

I am a freelance writer with twenty years' experience of developing training courses and materials for a worldwide audience. After many years' working in the corporate world, I now have my own company, Words on Words, which has earned a high reputation for clear and creative content.

Two decades of corporate life have given me keen insights into the value of teams and teamworking and I have collaborated on a book on the business value of team-building events. Author of *WoW Entrepreneur – How To Start Your Own Business*, I bring experience of teamworking, marketing, selling skills, change management and customer satisfaction gained in the course of my work for clients in the financial, automotive, retail, IT and telecommunications sectors.

With an Honours degree from Oxford University in Psychology and Philosophy and a knowledge of four European languages, my career includes many local, European and global training projects which have taken me to Europe, North America and the Far East.

In one minute

As a team leader, do you believe you can make a real difference to the performance of your team? If you do, *Create a Winning Team* will help you do just that and if you don't, then this book might just change your mind!

You need to focus on five success factors as a team leader: creating a balanced team; setting clear objectives; focusing on the outcomes; keeping the team motivated; and recognizing and rewarding good performance.

Creating a balanced team helps achieve objectives and desired outcomes. When you know the different personality types of your team you can assign them to the role that suits them best.

You will want to consider the skills you need for your development and aim to build on the four core team leader skills of listening, communicating, building trust and planning.

You will also want to consider the development needs of the team and may want to look at providing some form of team-building activity. This can be helpful both for teams who are performing well and for those whose performance is poor.

How do you communicate to your team and they to you? Meetings, e-mail and one-on-one sessions all have their place. It's a matter of knowing which one to use when.

Finally, be focused, be confident, be positive and you will create your winning team.

1

You and teamwork

In this chapter you will learn:
- **who this book is for**
- **how to use this book**
- **how to identify the teams in your life.**

Who is this book for?

Most of you, no matter what field you work in, will have worked as part of a team at one time or another. Many of you will have led teams, whether it's in business, the health service, education, the arts, the voluntary sector, your own business or some other area.

Create a Winning Team is aimed at team leaders who have been newly thrust into the role and want to become the best team leader ever or existing team leaders who want to improve their skills.

THE CHALLENGE

A team leader is one who guides and inspires others. Yet becoming a team leader can often create mixed feelings in people.

For example:

▶ your self-esteem is raised -- but some colleagues may resent you for having been given this role

▶ you find yourself in the position of leading a team of people who just last week were your colleagues

▶ you enjoy the increased responsibility – but the pressures on your time are even greater

▶ you want to earn respect – but some members of your team are more senior to you.

These situations can be resolved and you already possess many of the qualities necessary to handle any potential areas of conflict.

Here's a typical example. Read through it and think about what your response would be as you read the rest of the book.

I have recently been promoted to team leader in the marketing department of a leading IT company in the UK. I lead a team of ten people of mixed abilities, motivation and ambition. I'm having a few teething problems.

The first is my relative youth. I'm only 22 and while two of my team members are younger than me, the others are older, some considerably so, ranging from 24 to 35. Before my promotion I was just one of the team and I'm finding it difficult to get the older ones to trust my ability and respect my new position. Even the younger ones try it on and try to push the boundaries.

How do I assert my new authority without coming over too bossy and making the situation worse?

I do have two team members who are excellent and who produce great work. I tend to spend more time developing them to take on more responsibility. But then the other team members feel neglected and the quality of their work falls off.

I'm not sure I should be prepared to develop those team members who aren't performing to standard. It's a dilemma.

I'd greatly appreciate any advice you can offer.

Suggested solutions to the case study above are given in Chapter 10 but do resist the temptation to jump straight there now. Take advantage of all the advice and tips that lie along the way first so you are in the best position to offer solutions to these difficult but typical situations for new young team leaders.

Create a Winning Team is designed to give those of you who find yourselves in these or similar situations practical advice and guidance from the start. In addition it includes:

Insight boxes: At regular intervals throughout the text, insight boxes have been added to highlight a special idea or thought worth noting. Insight boxes give you pause for reflection.

Exercise boxes: From time to time you will find an exercise box at the end of a section. This will invite you to do something yourself. It may be to consider what you have just read and apply it to yourself or your team. Their purpose is to provide some interactivity and to get you thinking for yourself.

Keys to a winning team: At the end of each chapter, 'Things to remember' provides a handy summary of the key points from the preceding chapter. These will help you fix the main issues of each chapter in your mind for the future.

Voice of direct experience: Throughout the book, in context, you will hear comments from the direct experience of team leaders of different ages from a wide variety of sectors and roles. These include banking, community project direction, air traffic control, the RAF, urban art projects and even dance. As wide a range of voices as possible has been included with examples beyond the world of business to give variety. Hearing at first hand the experiences of young team leaders in their own words is the best kind of learning and balances the more theoretical parts of this book. Whatever your role or sector you can expect to find resonances with the experiences quoted here.

Models: Models help to pin down ideas and give them shape and structure such as 'Cog's Ladder', deBono's 'Six Thinking Hats', Tuckman's 'Storming, Forming, Norming, Performing', Drexler and Sibbet's 'Team Performance Model', Hersey and Blanchard's 'Situational Leadership Theory' and so on.

Insight

Where models are included they are all explained in easy-to-understand terms, in line with the promise of this book to be practical and down to earth.

What you will learn

Most people are in a team of one kind or another. This may be at work, with your family, or in your social or sporting lives. Wherever you are involved with more than two other people you are likely to be in a team. The popular expression 'Team X' as used, for example, in 'Team GB' or more recently (at the time of writing) in 'Team Middleton', implies that sense of being together in something more than just a group of individuals. It means belonging to a larger entity.

Exercise

▶ To how many teams do you belong?
▶ Take a moment now to think of the different teams of which you are a member.
▶ See the end of this chapter for examples.

This book is about teams, about being in teams and especially about leading teams. If you are leading a team you will want to be successful in that role and win the trust and respect of your team members. Here you can learn the steps you need to take to create a winning team.

Working as a team means you can be much more effective than working alone. This is why teamworking is so popular and effective. How to work successfully as a team is the theme of this book.

The chapters in *Create a Winning Team* provide practical answers to the following key questions:

How do you:

▶ understand what teams do?
▶ become a successful team leader?
▶ create a balanced team?
▶ work as a team?
▶ make your team succeed?
▶ improve your teamwork skills?
▶ develop the team?
▶ find the right way to talk to your team?
▶ create a winning team?

The contents are designed both as a narrative which you can profitably read through chapter by chapter from beginning to end, or as separate sections that you can select and dip into when you want or need to seek out specific information for reference.

WHAT THIS BOOK COVERS

What teams do

Answers basic questions about teamwork:

▶ What is a team and what do they do?
▶ Why do you have teams?
▶ When are teams effective?
▶ What's the right size for the team?

It covers the groundwork by defining key terms and sets the scene for what follows.

It gives the reasons for teams, the criteria for being effective as a team and why a team leader is important.

How to become a successful team leader

The first questions to be answered are 'What is a leader?' and 'Why are team leaders needed?'

▶ What skills do you need, particularly when you're a new team leader?
▶ What does it take to be a successful team leader?
▶ What's the right way to behave?
▶ How does acting assertively produce positive results?
▶ How should you deal with difficult behaviour?

Different styles of team leadership are described to show which produce the best results. Situational Leadership Theory is introduced as a model.

How to create a balanced team

As a team leader, knowing the different personality types of the team and the role that suits them best helps build a powerful team. An explanation is given as to why it is really helpful to assess the personality profiles of the team.

Four of the most popular techniques available to do this are summarized here:

▶ Belbin®
▶ MBTi®
▶ SDI®
▶ *Psycho*-Geometrics®

Psycho-Geometrics® is a more recent technique. It assigns people's personalities to one of five symbolic shapes and describes how different shapes interact with each other.

You will learn how to create a balanced team by assigning team members to roles that match their personality profiles.

How to work as a team
When the team is new, what are the considerations? It's an opportunity but also a challenge when you start from scratch.

What happens when the team already exists? The methods of working with an existing team are explored.

For both, the real challenge is to win team member trust and confidence plus respect for you as team leader.

Other types of team and their characteristics are described, e.g. independent and interdependent.

Teams go through stages in their development. Two models are considered, Charrier's 'Cog's Ladder' and Tuckman's 'Storming, Forming, Norming, Performing'.

De Bono's 'Six Thinking Hats' provides a tool to help teams think together more effectively.

How to help your team succeed
The key message is that a good team leader can make a real difference to the team's performance. In considering the actions needed to lead a team successfully, answers are given to the questions:

- ▶ What does success feel like?
- ▶ Why is it important to set objectives and focus on results?
- ▶ What is the role of motivation?
- ▶ How can you best reward and recognize team members for their efforts?

How to improve your teamwork skills
What are the social skills needed by team leaders and members alike to function effectively in a team?

Four key skills or attributes needed to be an effective team leader are detailed:

- listening
- communicating
- building trust
- planning.

These skills are described in detail plus a range of additional skills are summarized.

How to develop your team

Team members have their own needs for development both individually and collectively but what investment of time is needed to improve the team? Here you will find help on:

- how to maximize the team's potential
- how to develop yourself
- the pros and cons of team-building activities and events
- developing the team on no or very little budget
- what happens when the team isn't working.

For new teams and changing teams, well chosen team-building activities can help bond the team together, for example:

- when the team is performing well, how an event can be seen as a reward.
- when it's performing badly, how an event can be a diagnostic and a corrective.

How to find the right way to talk to your team

This chapter's about the best ways to communicate and take decisions. How do you get the message across most effectively and by what means? It answers questions about:

- when and how to hold meetings
- how to write effective e-mails
- how to use one-on-one communication.

When should you use which method of communication? How do you manage the team's time in an efficient manner? How often should you hold meetings? Does everyone need to be there all the time?

How to create a winning team

The conclusion draws together all the key themes. It provides:

- suggested solutions to the issues raised at the start of the book
- final words of advice to the team leader in terms of being confident, focused and positive
- the launch pad to make a real difference to the team and the organization
- the means to create a winning team.

> **Exercise: team leader characteristics**
> Now think about the characteristics you believe a successful team leader should possess and make a list. You can find our suggestions at the end of the next chapter.

List of teams

Here's our list of different types of team. How many teams do you belong to?

At work
- Everyday work teams
- Business strategy teams
- Taskforce teams
- Cross-functional teams, e.g. HR, risk assessment
- Quality circle teams
- Customer service teams
- Maintenance teams
- Sales teams
- One-off project teams
- Teams for special events and parties
- Self-managed teams.

At home
- Nuclear family
- Extended family meeting, e.g. Christmas and special occasions.

Social life
- Sports teams
- Drama or music clubs or societies
- Religious teams, e.g. church flowers, churchyard maintenance.

2

What teams do

In this chapter you will learn:
- *how to find the answers to some of the basic questions about teamwork*
- *how you define a team and what teams are for*
- *why you should work as a team and what type of team or group you belong to*
- *when to consider when a team is not a team.*

What is a team?

From the RAF Officer:

> *When the task requires the activities of more than one person. This could be for two reasons; the workload is too high for one person or the requirements demand different skills requiring different people.*

TEAM = Together Everyone Achieves More

Here is an excellent definition of a team:

> *A small number of people with complementary skills who are committed to a common purpose, performance objectives and approach for which they hold themselves mutually accountable.*
>
> Katzenbach and Smith

The key elements of the team:

A small number of people	An organization or a division can never be a team. Research shows the optimum team size is five to seven team members, though this depends on the team's purpose.
Complementary skills	A team comprising people with all the same skills will not work. A team needs a balance of skills so it can draw on a range and depth of experience.
Committed to a common purpose, performance objectives and approach	A team differs from a group because its members are bound together in sharing common objectives and purpose. A group lacks the same commitment and shared approach.
They hold themselves mutually accountable	A team acts 'all for one and one for all' with a shared responsibility for good and bad results. They do not take individual blame or credit but act collectively.

Insight

A 2003 HOW-FAIR survey revealed that Americans think 'being a team player' was the most important factor in getting ahead in the workplace. This was ranked higher than several factors, including 'merit and performance', 'leadership skills', 'intelligence', 'making money for the organization' and 'long hours'.

http://teamwork.askdefine.com/

WHEN IS A TEAM NOT A TEAM?

A team, then, works collaboratively to achieve a shared and common goal. Most groups of any kind do need to collaborate for one reason or another. However, not all groups need to collaborate as much as the tight knit team in the definition.

Teams are characterized by interdependence, communication, co-ordination and shared activities, while groups lack these qualities.

Insight
Some people use the word 'team' when they really mean 'employees'. A 'sales team' is a common example of this loose usage where 'sales staff' is a more precise description of the typical arrangement.

WHICH TYPE OF TEAM, OR GROUP, DO YOU BELONG TO?

A group is not a team. Teams are able to maximize their strengths and minimize their weaknesses because their skills complement each other and they can combine their energy to create a whole that is larger than its parts.

Team members need to learn how to help one another and help other team members realize their true potential so they can create an environment that allows everyone to go beyond their limitations.

Members in a successful team:

▶ recognize their interdependence and understand that both personal and team objectives are best accomplished with mutual support; time is not wasted over individual territory or seeking personal gain at the expense of others

- feel a sense of ownership for their jobs because they are committed to objectives they helped to establish
- contribute to the organization's success by applying their unique talent and knowledge to team objectives
- work in a climate of trust and are encouraged to express openly ideas, opinions, disagreements and feelings; questions are welcomed
- practise open and honest communication; they make an effort to understand each other's point of view
- are encouraged to develop skills and apply what they learn on the job; they receive the support of the team.
- work to resolve conflict quickly and constructively; they recognize conflict as normal but view such situations as opportunities for new ideas and creativity rather than as a threat
- recognize and comment on good work carried out by other members of the team, knowing that their own good work will be similarly acknowledged by their peers.

HOW A GROUP DIFFERS FROM A TEAM

In a group, on the other hand, you are more likely to find individuals who:

- work at cross purposes with others
- focus on themselves because they have not helped plan their group's objectives
- are told what to do and whose suggestions are not encouraged
- place little trust in others' motives and view disagreements as divisive
- play games, set communication traps and are overly cautious about what they say
- are limited in how far they can apply whatever training they receive
- find themselves in conflicts which they do not know how to resolve
- consider conforming to be more important than achieving positive results.

Much of the time, you may work on your own or be dealing with a customer rather than a colleague. It's important to realize that you are not in a team all the time. Senior team leaders will run their own departments most of the time but meet together with other senior team leaders for a monthly meeting for the duration of which they are a team, e.g. Finance Director and Sales Director, etc.

The principles of good teamworking are well established and well documented. They will be summarized in the next chapter. But remember that this is just the starting point. The real challenge is how well you put these principles into practice. This book is here to lead you in the right direction. Let its practical, down to earth, no nonsense wisdom be your guide.

You can make a difference.

Insight

Remember at all times that, as a team leader, you can make a real difference to your team and your organization. You can help create a winning team.

This is the mantra of this book. Read, inwardly digest, place it on your wall, commit it to memory and believe in your heart that no matter how great the obstacles or how heavy the load, you can and will make a real difference.

Why work as a team?

Working together works.

Dr Robert Gilbert, corporate trainer

When you work as a team you get more done, you work more effectively and you can do bigger projects. These are the key benefits of teamworking.

Thomas Edison claimed, 'I'd do it on my own if I could,' but the truth is you just can't do that in today's interdependent business world. A team can contribute more ideas and offer more experience than someone working on their own.

Successful teams achieve more positive results by allowing team members:

▶ to take part in decision making
▶ to contribute more fully towards shared objectives
▶ to share in their team's success.

These actions help them reach their objectives. This is particularly true for customer service initiatives. If customers are to receive the desired level of service, then this depends on the team working together.

As an individual team member, you have your own contribution to make in terms of knowledge, skill, creativity, commitment and attitude; as an individual, you think, feel and respond according to your personality.

Insight

How much stronger therefore will your contribution be when you lend your support and co-operation to others to achieve a common goal?

As an example, let's consider a sports team. Clearly, some players will have more talent than others, but in the end they will not be successful as a team unless they are motivated to work towards a common goal. A good team leader (in this context a manager or a coach) will help them by training them to play together, making allowances for the individual team members' strengths and weaknesses. The need for a balanced team is discussed in Chapter 4.

With teamworking, the results achieved are seldom the outcome of one individual's talent. Each person is influenced by the attitude and actions of colleagues and team leaders. A positive influence produces a productive workplace and vice versa.

While the concept of teamwork is easy to understand, its application takes dedication and effort. *Create a Winning Team* will provide you with the advice and tools you need to improve your performance and become a successful team leader.

When, how and why are teams effective?

From the Air Traffic Controller:

Teams are at their most effective when the objectives are made clear by the team leader and when the team members are made to feel that they make a positive contribution to the outcome. Teams are least effective when the members are at odds over the method of achieving an outcome; this is often because the team leader has not been monitoring progress and directing activities when necessary.

WHEN ARE TEAMS EFFECTIVE?

Teams work best when they have a clearly defined goal and purpose. Additionally, teams work well and achieve the best results when team members are:

▶ open minded
▶ flexible
▶ experienced
▶ prepared to use their skills and knowledge to the full.

On the other hand, teams do not work well when team members:

▶ do not co-operate
▶ do not listen to what other team members have to say
▶ do not share a common purpose
▶ do not trust their fellow team members.

A stable team is important – a team with a constantly changing line up is likely to perform poorly. When team members constantly drop out or change the rest of the team suffers. Teams work best when the members in the team remain the same for the duration of the project or longer if it's a permanent team.

Bringing a new team member on board can have an unsettling effect on the balance of the existing team and you will have to go through the time consuming process of assimilating the new member into the team. See 'How teams develop' in Chapter 5.

HOW ARE TEAMS EFFECTIVE?

The emotional strength of the team comes first. According to John Frost, Managing Director of Values Based Leadership, emotional strength is crucial to the team's successful performance. This strength is based on the trust and communication that exists between team members.

Of course, roles and objectives are important but it is emotional strength that comes first and which really binds a team together to create a great performance.

What is emotional strength? It's made up of a number of factors that consistently deliver results. These are:

▶ trust
▶ communication

- ▶ emotional resilience
- ▶ leadership.

Other factors do come into play and teams certainly do need to understand their objectives and the role they have to carry out. They do need to know their function and their key targets. They do need to understand how they can best support the objectives of their team members.

However, even with very clear targets and at an early stage of development, it's been shown that teams do not deliver against those targets. Frost's argument is not that they don't understand what they have to do to get results. Rather, it's that they have not put the energy into how they have to be. This is because they have not first developed emotional strength.

Frost quotes Drexler and Sibbet's *Team Performance Model* (1999) where goals, roles and deliverables are only considered after the key emotional strengths that will bind the team together and sustain performance are developed.

The Team Performance Model has three key stages:

1 orientation
2 trust
3 leadership.

Stage 1 – Orientation

Orientation is partly about the 'Why am I here?' question and mainly about values. It covers the team's purpose and how the team will contribute to the business. It discusses the team's identity and values and how team members need to align with these values.

It asks:

- ▶ Does your team have a set of values which act as a guide for decision-making?
- ▶ What values do you use to measure individual performance as well as profitability – team or company?

Values are the glue that binds the team together. A team that is aligned with its values is a powerful unit.

Stage 2 – Trust

This is about building and creating mutual trust, respect and support for each other. Trust has a direct link to performance. Without trust, a team will always underperform. Trust requires emotional resilience.

As Stephen M. R. Covey points out in *The Speed of Trust* (Simon & Schuster, 2006) that when trust is high, the speed at which the team performs increases and therefore its costs reduce and it becomes more profitable.

Exercise

Ask yourself:

- ▶ What is the level of trust in your team right now?
- ▶ What does it feel like working in your team?
- ▶ Is it a positive or a negative experience?
- ▶ Where do you spend your time and energy – on value added activities or worrying about the quality of the relationships in the team?

Trust is based on open and honest communication, and communication is the key to creating trust. It's a virtuous circle where the one helps to create the other. This builds support and confidence in the team. For more detail, see 'Build trust' in Chapter 7.

Communication then means being open and honest and telling team members the truth they need to hear. You often underestimate people by assuming you will hurt their feelings if you are honest with them. The reality is you are only protecting yourself. The team will underperform if team members are not open and honest not just about what they think but also about how they feel.

None of this is easy but the art of tough conversations, when mastered, has a dramatic effect on a team's performance. Only by naming the elephant in the room can you have a chance of dealing with it! Communication is described in more detail in Chapter 7.

Emotional resilience is about how the team responds to setbacks and how it learns from those set backs. To develop this key competence, a team needs strong relationships and the support that goes with them. A resilient team will review what happens and have an open and honest discussion. It will not lay the blame at anyone's door but will make a change that leads to improved performance.

Stage 3 – Leadership
Leadership is the final stage in developing teams. While team leaders cannot create a high performing team on their own, they can be responsible for the team not performing. The key role for the team leader is to help the team create the culture and the climate that releases the team members' full potential so they can perform to the highest level of their ability.

Leadership is an art and those who practise it best tend to have three key emotional qualities:

1 Courage: the courage to do the right thing even when it is hard.
2 Persistence: the ability to recover from a setback, learn and refocus on your vision.
3 Humility: the understanding that you are there to serve others rather than to take all the glory.

Being a good team leader means being able to admit your mistakes. It means being humble without being arrogant or proud. This kind of leadership engages the heart as well as the head. Leadership is described in more detail in Chapter 3.

Without exception, the teams that sustain performance over time are the ones that invest in the emotional foundations first. They understand that when the emotional connection is made, when the team decides what it wants to be, then achieving what it wants to do follows naturally.

John Frost, *Values Based Leadership Ltd, HR Initiatives Newsletter 2009*
Adapted from John Frost, Managing Director, Values Based Leadership Ltd
http://www.hrinitiatives.co.uk/March_2009.pdf

You've seen the fundamental importance of trust to teamwork success. Consider now what happens if that trust is damaged or destroyed.

Teamworking and trust

Trust is something that takes time to build but that can be destroyed in minutes. So what do you need to be alert to in order to avoid trust being destroyed?

Not following up: If you have said to team members that they are expected to deliver something specific by a certain time and date, you need to make sure that you follow up. People will interpret failing to follow up as if you don't care or will think what you ask them to do is not important.

Favouritism: If you are part of a team, there are going to be people that you connect with better than others. It can be really tempting to treat those who you connect with differently to others. Don't do this as you will create divisions.

Not delivering: If you, as the leader of the team, made certain commitments, then make sure you deliver on them. You set the tone for the rest of the team. If you have a reputation for non-delivery, others will follow suit.

Publicly criticizing: The best laid plans don't always come off. There may have been several people who contributed to the poor outcome or whose lack of contribution led to a less than ideal outcome. Deal with this behind closed doors rather than publicly.

Not dealing with toxic behaviour: People will, if you allow them, take advantage. If their behaviours are toxic, they will bring down the whole team eventually. When you notice toxic behaviour, deal with it.

Adapted from Duncan Brodie's, *5 things that destroy trust*
http://ezinearticles.com/?Team-Working—5-Things-That-Destroy-Trust&id=5248019

Now you're getting to the heart of how teams are effective.

First you need to recognize the importance of emotional strength made up of trust, communication, emotional resilience and leadership. If this is not established first, other things fail. It's like having shaky foundations for your house which causes the whole building to be unsound. Roles, functions and targets must all build upon the foundation of emotional strength if they are to succeed.

WHAT ARE THE NEXT ESSENTIAL BUILDING BLOCKS TO MAKE AN EFFECTIVE TEAM?

The following is adapted from: *Leading Change* by John P. Kotter; Harvard Business School Press, 1996 (See http://www.opm.gov/perform/articles/2000/aug00-5.asp). John P. Kotter, the distinguished professor and author, has spent his life at Harvard Business School writing and teaching about leadership and change. In his book, *Leading Change*, (Harvard Business School Press, 1996), Kotter states that teams built on mutual trust and respect can thrive during organizational change if they possess the following five attributes:

- ▶ shared vision
- ▶ shared responsibilities
- ▶ continuous learning and development
- ▶ customer focus
- ▶ capability to gather and use feedback.

Although they may seem common sense, many teams fail to incorporate them. When this happens, minor and major changes catch teams off guard, undermine their productivity and often cause them to question their purpose, feel defensive or just crumble.

Shared vision
Establishing a shared vision is critical because it coordinates the actions of individual members toward agreed upon objectives. The shared vision should be:

- ▶ easily understood and communicated
- ▶ able to support the team's efforts to provide better products or services to customers
- ▶ desirable, focused, feasible and supported by the team.

This shared vision gives team members a clear sense of direction. They can focus on trying to make things better, not worse. It means they don't have to check in with management all the time.

Shared responsibilities

Successful teams develop shared responsibilities which allow team members to address change actively.

▶ Successful teams share responsibilities and hold each other accountable for the team's performance. This encourages team members to share issues and concerns with the team.

▶ Team members support changes in work assignments, resources, and priorities when they realize it will aid in the team's performance.

▶ Team members learn to value each other's talents and how to maximize them.

Continuous learning

Ongoing learning for team members is also critical. Some high-performance teams spend as much as 30 per cent of their time in training on such subjects as:

▶ team building
▶ leadership
▶ communication
▶ coaching
▶ technical knowledge
▶ computer skills
▶ problem-solving
▶ budget process
▶ conflict resolution
▶ critical thinking and writing.

See Chapter 7 'How to improve your teamwork skills'.

> ### Exercise
> How effective is your continuous learning? Ask yourself the questions below:
>
> ▶ When did you last receive training in one of these areas?
> ▶ Which topic did it concern?
> ▶ How useful was it for you?
> ▶ How helpful was it for the team?
> ▶ How recently have you used that training?

This systematic training breeds a feeling of *esprit de corps* or team spirit. Each team member feels equally important to the team and responsible for improving both technical and interpersonal skills. Most importantly, team members are given the opportunity to use the skills they learn immediately after the training takes place.

Customer focus

Successful teams pay attention to their customers and focus on customer requirements, satisfaction and complaints. Teams can continuously improve performance by using:

- ▶ customer satisfaction surveys
- ▶ performance objectives
- ▶ informal recommendations from internal and external customers.

Feedback and data

Successful teams meet often to review current performance and develop improvement plans using clear performance measures. For example, using weekly or monthly data from customer satisfaction measurement systems allows the team to direct its energy to reducing errors and to improving the quality or timeliness of its products or services.

Adapted from: *Leading Change* by John P. Kotter; Harvard Business School Press, 1996
http://www.opm.gov/perform/articles/2000/aug00-5.asp

Insight: Implications for the future

According to Kotter, teams like this will be needed throughout organizations. One executive cannot have the expertise to absorb rapidly shifting information. A team is needed to create the corporate vision and empower the workforce to meet fast-shifting challenges more effectively than a hierarchical executive staff.

On top of the foundation of emotional strength have been added the following essential building blocks. These show how teams need to:

- ▶ create a clear vision
- ▶ share responsibilities
- ▶ spare time for learning
- ▶ focus on customers
- ▶ monitor performance via data and feedback.

These are essential because without them teams can become ineffective and lose their way.

WHY ARE TEAMS EFFECTIVE?

To deliver quality service – both internal and external – requires teamwork. The team needs to work together if the service is to come together for customers. This means team members benefiting from the support and co-operation of their colleagues to achieve a common goal.

More is achieved collectively than individually. Remember that teams that work well make a huge impact and they benefit from the rewards that go with this impact.

Six reasons why teams are effective

1 Mutual support

Team members support each other. They will often go to great lengths when they know that they can rely on the team's encouragement. Especially when the going gets tough they will create a strong sense of camaraderie.

2 Contribution of knowledge to shared objectives

Team members have different skills and knowledge. By using all these aspects in a team, more ideas can be generated. More ideas then generate more creative solutions leading to better results.

3 Skill sharing

Even the best qualified team member can't do everything. Some people excel at coming up with the ideas while others love the detail. When a team works together it draws on a range of skills to deliver outstanding results.

4 Speed

Splitting up a project between team members means the work can move forward in parallel and the end result is reached much faster. When a project involves some research, a proposition, financing and implementation, one team member could take months or years to make it happen.

5 Satisfaction

Working as a team results in higher job satisfaction for the members. As people interact they generate more energy and enthusiasm. This energy translates into positive motivation producing successful results.

6 Sounding board
Other team members act as a sounding board when there are various options, testing and challenging suggestions and allowing only the best ideas to proceed.

Adapted from Duncan Brodie's *6 Key Benefits of Teamwork*
http://EzineArticles.com/?expert=Duncan_Brodie

Exercise

So how effective is teamwork in your workplace? Think about the qualities listed above.

Which are most important to you? What could you do to improve them?

What is the right size for a team?

This is not such an easy question to answer. The right team size for effective team performance is a much researched and debated topic. You need to consider a number of factors when determining the best team size.

These include the:

▶ requirements of the task to be accomplished
▶ purpose for forming the team
▶ expectations you have of the team and its members
▶ roles that the team members need to play
▶ amount of interconnectivity needed for optimal team performance
▶ team's function, activities and objectives.

While the best team size is not an easy answer, experience and research indicates that the optimum team size is five to seven team members and that a team can continue to function effectively with four to nine members. Teams are known to function cohesively with a size of up to 12 members.

Fewer than five members results in decreased perspectives and diminished creativity. Membership in excess of 12 results in increased conflict and greater potential of sub-groups forming.

Larger team sizes of up to 20 team members are possible where individual team members are not expected to form a cohesive, highly interconnected team. Larger teams are more likely to form sub-teams and working groups to accomplish the actual work of a project.

These larger groups are effective as examples for strategic planning input, overall project communication or building support for an idea.

Adapted from Heathfield, S. M. *About.com Guide*
http://humanresources.about.com/od/teambuildingfaqs/f/optimum-team-size.htm

Many teams go through a life cycle of stages, identified by Bruce Tuckman as: forming, storming, norming, performing and adjourning and by Charrier's 'Cog's Ladder'. See 'How do teams develop?' in Chapter 5.

Answer: group vs team exercise

Which would you say describes a group and which a team? If you had to put them on scale from 0 = group and 10 = team where would each one be?

1 Members work independently with no requirement to co-operate.
2 Little interdependence between members but they may learn from each other's experience.
3 All members must work together well, although each member has distinct areas of responsibility.
4 A highly interdependent team that needs to perform well to meet the organization's requirements.

▶ 1 & 2 describe groups and 3 & 4 describe teams.
▶ On scale of 1 to 10 where group = 0 and team = 10:

1 = 0, 2 = 2, 3 = 8, 4 = 10

Suggested answers: team leader characteristics

Here's our list for the characteristics of a successful team leader. How did your list compare?

A successful team leader is someone who is:

▶ a communicator
▶ trusted
▶ respected
▶ motivated and able to motivate others
▶ skilled in delegating
▶ determined and committed
▶ loyal to the team and the organization
▶ a listener
▶ encouraging and co-operative
▶ flexible and adaptable
▶ sensitive to the needs and views of others
▶ genuinely interested in the development of others.

You may know someone who embodies all these qualities but it's rare for one person to possess them all. This should not prevent you from aspiring to acquire them.

KEYS TO A WINNING TEAM

What is a team?

A small number of people with complementary skills who are committed to a common purpose, performance objectives and approach for which they hold themselves mutually accountable.

Katzenbach and Smith

Teams maximize their strengths and minimize their weaknesses because:

- their skills complement each other

- they combine their energy to create a whole that is larger than its parts

- a group does not constitute a team; a group usually lacks mutual support, a shared sense of ownership and the pursuit of a common goal.

Why work as a team?

- You get more done, you work more effectively and you can do bigger projects.

- Each person is influenced by the attitude and actions of colleagues and team leaders.

When is a team effective?

Teams achieve the best results:

- when they have a clearly defined goal and purpose

- when team members are open minded, flexible and experienced.

How is a team effective?

Emotional strength:

- really binds a team together to create great performance

- consists of trust, communication, emotional resilience and leadership.

Why is a team effective?

Because there is:

- mutual support

- contribution of knowledge to shared objectives

- skill sharing

- speed.

What is the right size for a team?

- It depends on the team's objective but is typically five to seven members.

3

How to become a successful team leader

In this chapter you will learn:
- *how to become an effective leader*
- *how to lead your team successfully*
- *what kind of behaviour to adopt and how to deal with the difficult behaviour of others.*

What is leadership and why is a team leader needed?

WHAT IS LEADERSHIP?

What are the key factors you need to lead a team? Consider the next two items.

Six factors that drive confidence in leaders

For the past few years, the Harvard Kennedy School's Center for Public Leadership has conducted an annual public opinion poll to determine the sector leaders in which Americans have the most and least confidence and the factors behind those confidence levels. The 2009 results showed some interesting conclusions. According to the study, there are six key factors that have the greatest impact on Americans' confidence in their leaders. These factors are:

- **trust** in what the leaders say
- **competence** to do the job
- working for the **greater good** of society
- share my **values**
- get good **results**
- **in touch** with people's needs and concerns.

http://www.centerforpublicleadership.org

Now the second item:

Traits of effective leaders

Leaders exist at all levels of an organization. At the edges of the enterprise, of course, leaders are accountable for less territory. Their vision may sound more basic; the number of people to motivate may be two. But they perform the same leadership role as their more senior counterparts. They excel at seeing things through fresh eyes and at challenging the status quo. They are energetic and seem able to run through or around, obstacles...

However, the most notable trait of great leaders is their quest for learning. They show an exceptional willingness to push themselves out of their own comfort zones... Often they are driven by goals or ideals that are bigger than what any individual can accomplish...

Leaders invest tremendous talent, energy, and caring in their change efforts, yet few see the results they had hoped for... All institutions need effective leadership, but nowhere is the need greater than in the organization seeking to transform itself.

Adapted from John P. Kotter. *Leader to Leader*, (Drucker Foundation and Jossey–Bass Inc., 1998)

To summarize Kotter's argument, at the more extreme end of the scale, outstanding leaders, especially lower down the organization, are likely to:

- challenge the status quo
- demonstrate a quest for learning
- pursue bigger goals than any individual can accomplish
- show talent, energy and caring.

Thinking about both these quotations, how many of the characteristics mentioned do you feel you have?

Do you inspire trust? Are you in touch with people's needs?

Do you see things through fresh eyes? Can you run through or around, obstacles? How far along Kotter's scale are you?

Take a moment to reflect before reading on about leadership.

There are three types of leadership according to John Adair, *Develop Your Leadership Skills* (Kogan Page, 2007). These are:

- assigned leadership (leader determined by their qualities)
- situation leadership (leader emerges from the situation)
- 'leaderless' leadership (no appointed leader so the team rules).

Assigned leadership
Assigned leadership stresses those **qualities** that belong to the individual alone, without taking into account the situation or the team. These can include qualities like:

- enthusiasm
- integrity
- toughness
- fairness
- warmth
- humility
- confidence.

Historical and charismatic leaders, particularly wartime leaders such as Napoleon or Churchill, are often seen in this light.

Situation leadership

The second approach to leadership stresses the idea that leadership emerges from the *situation* and plays down the importance of personal leadership qualities: 'Cometh the moment, cometh the man'.

Insight

A person may be a strong leader in one situation but not in another. Winston Churchill was an outstanding wartime leader but less successful in peace time. Or compare Gordon Brown's period as Chancellor of the Exchequer with his time as Prime Minister.

A situation leader needs individual knowledge linked to authority.

'Leaderless' leadership

The third approach to leadership is leaderless teams where the work is shared, with no one taking the overall leadership role, and so is very democratic. The focus is on getting the job done where leadership is shared and all members of the team show a high level of responsibility.

This team approach to leadership is common with some organizations having flatter management structures or with matrix management where different people take the lead for different tasks at different times, according to their skills and knowledge. See 'Self-managed teams' in Chapter 5.

> *A leader is best when people barely know he exists, when his work is done, his aim fulfilled, they will say: we did it ourselves.*
>
> Lao Tzu

A leader is someone who can get the job done

Over the last few decades, the trend has been to move away from charismatic leadership or the 'great man' theory (referred to above as 'assigned leadership'), which defined leadership as one who leads by force of personality and big speeches. Now leaders tend to be defined more as people who can get the job done.

Insight: Appearances can deceive

Some leaders are strident and forceful while others exude a quiet confidence. A loud voice is not always a sign of confidence. In fact, those who appear outwardly the most forceful and confident are often actually covering a lack of confidence.

A better indicator of confidence is effectiveness. An effective leader gets the task done on time, understands the rules and achieves a successful outcome. Use of management speak or over complication indicates a lack of confidence. It takes strength to simplify.

Followership

A leader is one who is followed. Wherever there are leaders there will also be followers. Followership is the other side of the coin from leadership and a successful team needs followers as well as leaders. A team made up solely of leaders will not function. Like leadership, followership is a skill. There is a Leader–Follower feedback loop where leaders create followers who in turn create leaders.

According to David Straker, from the follower's perspective, there are four basic reasons to be a follower:

1 Respect: Both the leader and the solution are important to me.
2 Trust: I will follow someone I trust.
3 Liking: I will follow someone I like.
4 Support: I will follow someone who supports me.

For a fuller account see: www.theleadershiphub.com/blogs/changing-minds-group-different-kinds-followership-and-how-they-help-define-leadership

So followership interacts with leadership. Good leaders create good followers and vice versa. This can be seen very clearly in teamwork where the strength and performance of the team are due to the qualities of the followers as much as the leader. Without followers, leaders have no one to lead.

From these theories, let's draw some conclusions about leadership as it tends to be practised in the contemporary business environment.

Leadership:

- is best defined as what you do rather than what you are
- is action-centred
- concerns the 'why' as well as the 'what'
- relies heavily on effective communication.

A leader:

- ▶ is someone who can get the job done
- ▶ has no one to lead without followers
- ▶ can be defined as one who guides and inspires others.

WHY IS A TEAM LEADER NEEDED?

Inventories can be managed, but people must be led.

H. Ross Perot

While it is sometimes possible to have self-managed teams without team leaders, the evidence is very much that you do need team leaders. See 'Self-managed teams' in Chapter 5.

The main reason for needing a team leader has to be focus. One person needs to be responsible for the overall objectives. On a big project with many different strands you need someone to pull it all together. It means you can allocate each separate part to someone else and they don't have to think about the whole picture. They can concentrate on their own task leaving the big picture to the team leader. So it's definitely helpful to have a team leader, though their style can vary a great deal.

Ackoff and Addison make the case for the difference a good team leader can make:

The extraordinary thing is the transformation that can take place when a good team leader arrives on the scene. The working atmosphere changes. Team members feel free to say what they think, to express ideas, to voice criticisms and to ask for change. The tone of meetings changes. Work improves. People get on together and work more co-operatively. It's the cheapest and fastest way to bring about a real change in the organization's culture.

Ackoff & Addison, *A Little Book Of F-Laws – 13 Common Sins Of Management*
(Triarchy Press, 2006)

Here are eight reasons why you need a team leader. They:

1 provide purpose
2 establish shared ownership for the results
3 develop team members to their fullest potential

4 make the work interesting and engaging
5 motivate and inspire team members
6 lead and facilitate constructive communication
7 monitor but not micromanage
8 build a star team, not a team of stars.

How a team leader saved the day and made things run better

In a stage production, a team member was injured and had to be taken out of show. This meant the musical number had to be restaged. Without a team leader – the dance captain – the show would have been a mess. Everybody would have had their own ideas about what to do and gone off in different directions.

In this situation the team leader knew exactly what needed to be done and was the only person who knew. It was only by the team listening to the team leader and then co-operating to pull together that the situation was resolved and the show could go on.

What does it take to be a new team leader?

WHAT DOES BECOMING A TEAM LEADER FOR THE FIRST TIME INVOLVE?

'New team leaders may welcome extra responsibility but it comes with greater accountability,' says David Pardey, 'It's like two sides of a coin: you can't have one without the other.' His checklist for first-time leaders is designed to help them know what to expect from their new role and cope with the burden of being in the firing line.

You can't really know what it's like to be a team leader until you do it. It's not a role for which you can easily prepare. The parts that make up role are:

▶ responsibility – particularly for people and their performance
▶ finances – revenues in and costs out
▶ products or services – manufacturing, marketing and distribution as relevant
▶ physical resources – how used and maintained
▶ people's health and safety
▶ green issues – how the organization affects the environment.

This list is not complete and team leaders are very unlikely to be responsible for all these areas. While it may just be one or two at first, they may take on more as their experience grows.

WHAT'S HARD FOR THE NEW TEAM LEADER?

With new responsibility comes accountability which can make some new team leaders become overly controlling. When you become accountable for how other people do their jobs, it makes sense for you to make absolutely sure they are done properly. Unfortunately this isn't a good way to motivate and inspire people!

One of the hardest things for new team leaders to learn is how to trust people or, more acutely, how to judge how much to trust other people.

Lawrence Appley described team leadership as 'getting things done through people' and first-time team leaders need to focus their attention on making sure that they have the knowledge, the skills and, most importantly, the confidence to ensure that the right things are done, and done right, by other people.

The following checklist is designed to help new, first-time team leaders, focus on what they can do and, most importantly, what they can't, so that they can ask for help in becoming more effective in their role, as soon as possible. It is based around the three key areas of knowledge, skills and confidence.

1 Knowledge

▶ What systems and procedures, standards and rules apply to you and your area of responsibility, over which you have no control? What people and resources, systems and procedures, standards and rules do you have specific responsibility for and what limits apply to that responsibility?

▶ To whom, and how, are you accountable for your exercise of that responsibility?

▶ Who are the people you have responsibility for, what is their role and what are they like? What do they think about their work, what do they want to do and what do they want from you as their team leader?

▶ Who else will you work with, including suppliers and customers, colleagues and stakeholders, what do they want from you and how can they help you to do your job more effectively?

2 Skills

What strengths do you bring to your new role and what are your weaknesses? In particular, how effective are you at:

▶ Working with other people, motivating, developing, understanding and supporting them to do their job effectively?

▶ Communicating with other people (personally and in writing), and understanding other people's communications with you (especially the unvoiced messages that are often the most important)?

▶ Identifying, collecting and analysing data on key aspects of your role and using this to inform your decisions and your understanding of the areas you have responsibility for?

▶ Identifying your objectives and managing your own work to achieve them?

▶ Using your experiences to learn and improve your own performance?

3 Confidence

One of the biggest challenges for new team leaders is having the confidence to make decisions, especially in relation to people who you have worked with as an equal. To develop your confidence, consider the following:

▶ Are you honest about your feelings, to yourself as much as to others with whom you work? You should acknowledge any fear, anger or other emotions you feel and work through it, not try to bottle it up – that's part of becoming emotionally intelligent.

▶ Do you ask others for their opinions and advice? Don't try to do things on your own. Asking others shows respect and gives you better information on which to make decisions – if someone brings you a problem, ask them what they would do, and test out their ideas to help determine the best course of action.

▶ Do you feel embarrassed managing people you once worked alongside? How do they feel about it? Ask them and discuss this with them; don't try to pretend that it's not an issue, but bring it out into the open.

▶ How can you get feedback on your performance, from your line team leader and from those you manage? This will help you identify what you are doing well and what you might need to improve, so ask!

Pardey advises not to expect to come out as 100 per cent on each of these aspects of the role; if you do, you are either an amazing prodigy or you are fooling yourself – probably the latter. The most effective team leaders are those who are able to make sense of the world around them and their place in it. This checklist will help first-time team leaders develop themselves and live up to the confidence that their organization has placed in them.

For more details see Pardey, David, *Introducing Leadership* (Butterworth-Heinemann, 2006).

WHAT TO DO WHEN THINGS GO WRONG?

As a new team leader you will inevitably make mistakes from time to time as you learn. Bob Selden in his book *What To Do When You Become The Boss* (Business Plus, 2010) has some good questions to ask yourself before you take up your new role:

- ▶ When I make a mistake, how will I handle it?
- ▶ Who will I tell?
- ▶ Who will I turn to for advice / support?
- ▶ How will I make sure I learn from my mistakes so that I improve as a team leader?

What style of team leadership?

Over time, people's thinking about styles of leadership has shifted from a very directive to a highly participative approach; from one where the leader gives the orders and expects to be obeyed to one where team members are consulted at length before any decision is taken. Neither one is right (or wrong) all the time. It depends on the situation.

Insight

In an emergency situation like a fire in the building, it would be appropriate to be directive. Giving orders would lead to a more successful outcome than holding a meeting to decide what to do!

As a team leader you need to have a range of styles for different situations. You need to know which one to use for a particular occasion and in response to your team members' behaviour. The section in this chapter on 'Situational Leadership Theory' expands this theme.

BASIC LEADERSHIP STYLES

Four basic leadership styles are:

- ▶ autocratic
- ▶ bureaucratic
- ▶ laissez-faire
- ▶ democratic.

Currently the last two are the dominant styles.

AUTOCRATIC LEADERSHIP STYLE

No man will make a great leader who wants to do it all himself or get all the credit for doing it.

Andrew Carnegie

The autocratic leader holds onto as much power and authority as possible. Team members are not consulted and are not allowed to give any input. They just obey orders. Trust between leader and team is lacking, being replaced by threats and punishment. This style of leadership has very much gone out of fashion nowadays, at least in democratic cultures.

This makes the autocratic style seem very undesirable, but you should be aware of it as there are times when it's the best style to use. You might need to use it when there is limited time in which to make a decision (as in the fire example above), where new team members don't know which tasks to perform and need detailed instructions or quite simply where team members do not respond to any other leadership style.

Bureaucratic leadership style

You can lead a bureaucrat to water, but you can't make him think.

Ric Keller

The bureaucratic leader follows procedure and policy to the letter and so is more of an enforcer than a team leader. When an event or action is not covered by policy, they will defer to authority and ask for a decision from the next in the chain of command.

This 'by the book' style can work when the task is very procedural and includes performing routine, precise or delicate steps which can be defined by rules. The big disadvantage of the bureaucratic style is that the work becomes boring and team members only do what is expected.

Democratic leadership style

> *The human race divides ... into those who want people to be controlled and those who have no such desire.*
>
> Robert A. Heinlein

The democratic, or participative, leadership style encourages team members to contribute to decision-making and problem-solving. Team leaders keep the team informed about everything that affects their work. While they still have the final say, the team leader gathers information from the team members before making a decision.

Typically, the team leader will help team members evaluate their own performance, set objectives with the team, encourage personal development and recognize effort. This style does tend to be most successful with skilled and experienced team members and works best when there is a complex problem requiring a great deal of input to solve or when changes must be made that affect the team.

Avoid this style when there's not enough time to get everyone's input, the business can't afford mistakes or where employee safety is a critical concern...or when there's a fire in the building!

Laissez-faire leadership style

> *Don't tell people how to do things. Tell them what to do and let them surprise you with their results.*
>
> George S. Patton

The laissez-faire leadership style is the 'hands-off' style where the team leader provides little or no direction giving team members as much freedom as possible. Power is handed to the team members who must set the team's objectives, make decisions and solve problems on their own. This is similar to the concept of the self-managed team.

Clearly for this style to be effective, team members must be trustworthy, experienced, highly skilled and have the motivation to work successfully on their own. It works well with outside experts, specialists and consultants who need less direct supervision.

This style should not be used when the team feels it needs a leader or as a means for a team leader to shirk his/her responsibilities or where the team need regular feedback and thanks for the work. See 'Self-managed teams' in Chapter 5.

VARYING LEADERSHIP STYLE

There are three other factors that also influence which leadership style to use.

▶ The team leader's personal background: what personality, knowledge, values, ethics and experiences does the team leader have? What does he or she think will work?
▶ The employees being supervised: team members are individuals with different personalities and backgrounds. The leadership style that team leaders use will vary depending upon the individual team member and to what they will respond best.
▶ The company: the traditions, values, philosophy and concerns of the company will influence how a team leader acts.

> ## Exercise
> Which of the four styles do you think you practise? Or do you use a mix of styles?
>
> Take a moment to think about it before reading on.

SITUATIONAL LEADERSHIP THEORY

As the name implies, Situational Leadership Theory believes that different leadership styles are needed to match different situations so that that team leaders must have the flexibility to adapt their style to the situation they are in and the style of their follower. The model can be applied beyond those in leadership or management positions to everyday life.

The Hersey and Blanchard model

The best known example of Situational Leadership Theory was developed by Paul Hersey, author of *Situational Leader* and Ken Blanchard, the management guru, later famous for his *One Minute Manager* series. They created a model of situational leadership in the late 1960s in their work *Management of Organizational Behaviour*, (Pearson Education, 2007) that shows you how to analyse the needs of the situation and then adopt the most appropriate leadership style. The theory remains popular because it is simple to understand and works in most places for most people. The model is based on two concepts:

1 leadership style
2 development level.

Leadership style
Blanchard and Hersey describe leadership style in terms of the amount of direction and support the team leader provides to their followers. They categorized these leadership styles into four types, named S1 to S4:

| S3 Low direction/High support **Supporting** Support, motivate and empower | S2 High direction/High support **Coaching** Explain, persuade, guide, and train | (High) |
| S4 Low direction/Low support **Delegating** Gets involved when requested | S1 High direction/Low support **Directing** Inform, describe, direct and instruct | Support (Low) |

(Low)   Direction   (High)

S1: Directing leaders define the roles and tasks of the follower and supervise them closely. Decisions are made by the leader and announced, so communication is largely one-way. (Compare with autocratic style above.)

S2: Coaching leaders still define roles and tasks but seek ideas and suggestions from the follower. Decisions remain the leader's prerogative but communication is much more two-way. (Compare with democratic style above.)

S3: Supporting leaders pass day-to-day decisions, such as task allocation and processes, to the follower. The leader facilitates and takes part in decisions, but control is with the follower. (Compare with bureaucratic style above.)

S4: Delegating leaders are still involved in decisions and problem-solving, but control is with the follower. The follower decides when and how the leader will be involved. (Compare with laissez-faire style.)

No one style is considered best, nor should all team leaders aspire to a single style. Leaders need to be flexible and must adapt according to the situation. However, each leader tends to have a natural style and in applying the model needs to know his natural style.

Development levels

The most appropriate leadership style depends on the person being led – the follower. Blanchard and Hersey modified their model to include the development level of the follower. They believed that the team leader's chosen style should be based on the competence and commitment of their followers. They categorized the possible development of followers into four levels which they named D1 to D4:

D3 High competence/Variable commitment Experienced and capable, but may lack the confidence to go it alone	D2 Some competence/Low commitment Some relevant skills but unable to do the job without help	(Low)
D4 High competence/High commitment Experienced at the job and comfortable with their ability to do it well	D1 Low competence/High commitment Lack the skills for the job in hand, but eager to learn and willing to take direction	Commitment
(High) ← Competence → (Low)		(High)

Development levels are also situational. For example, I might be generally skilled, confident and motivated in my job but would still drop into Level D1 when faced, say, with a task requiring skills I don't possess. Many leaders are D4 when dealing with the day-to-day running of their department, but move to D1 or D2 when dealing with a sensitive employee issue.

Leadership/development matching

The leadership style (S1 - S4) of the team leader must correspond to the development level (D1 - D4) of the follower. And it is the leader who must adapt, not the follower. To get the most of situational leadership, a leader should be trained how to operate effectively in various leadership styles and learn how to recognize the development level of others.

Insight

It's a dynamic relationship where what matters is not your style or your team member's style but how they match together.

Hersey and Blanchard give two examples of mismatches to illustrate what happens when the leadership style is misaligned with the follower.

Mismatch scenario I:

A new person joins your team and you're asked to help him through the first few days. You sit him in front of a PC, show him a pile of invoices that need to be processed today and then excuse yourself to a meeting. He is at level D1 and you've adopted S4, an obvious mismatch. Everyone loses because the new person feels helpless and demotivated and you don't get the invoices processed.

Mismatch scenario II:

You're handing over your duties to an experienced colleague before you leave for a holiday. You've listed all the tasks that need to be done and given him a detailed set of instructions on how to carry out each one. He is at level D4, and you've adopted S1. The work will probably get done but your colleague will despise you for treating him like an idiot.

But if you leave instructions for your new colleague, they'll be grateful. Give your experienced colleague a quick chat and a few notes before you go on holiday and everything will be fine. By adopting the right style to suit the follower's development level, work gets done, relationships are built and most importantly, the follower's development level will rise, to everyone's benefit.

Hersey, P. and Blanchard, K. H., *Management of Organizational Behavior 3rd Edition – Utilizing Human Resources*, (New Jersey: Prentice Hall, 1977).

How to be assertive and deal with difficult people

Assertive behaviour will greatly contribute to your overall effectiveness as a team leader. You and your team will achieve your objectives because you will be working together.

Being assertive is:

▶ getting what you want, need or prefer without belittling or putting down your colleagues

▶ ensuring that the needs and wants of both parties are met

▶ not violating the rights of others.

What is meant by 'rights'?

▶ The right to ask for what you want (recognizing that others have the right to say no)

▶ The right to have your own opinions and values and to express them appropriately

▶ The right to say 'I don't know' or 'I don't understand'

▶ The right to make your own decisions and cope with the consequences

▶ The right, in some instances, to decline responsibility for other people's problems.

So how do you recognize assertiveness in people? Here are some of the obvious characteristics of assertive people:

▶ They use eye contact

- They hold themselves erect; they don't slouch or slump in the chair if they are leading a meeting
- They 'own' what they say, e.g. 'I'd like to suggest…', 'I've got an idea…'
- They also use 'co-operative phrases', e.g. 'What do you think?', 'Shall we…?'
- They use 'appropriate' behaviour, e.g. they are open about their feelings – be they positive or negative and they express annoyance constructively without reverting to aggression.

Aggressive people, on the other hand, must win at all costs, even at the expense of others. They use phrases like:

- 'You must'
- 'You will'
- 'I want'.

They have a negative effect on others because they intimidate, demotivate, create arguments and stifle initiative.

Passive or submissive people, on the other hand, just want to please and will avoid conflict at all costs. They are easily recognized because they:

- are nervous and hesitant
- are apologetic
- devalue their own needs.

Passive people keep quiet at meetings, sit in unobtrusive positions and rarely volunteer.

Exercise
Think about your own style of behaviour.

In the main is it assertive, aggressive or submissive?

If it is either aggressive or submissive, consider learning how to shift towards a more assertive style. Re-read the above section for guidelines on how to achieve this.

DEALING WITH DIFFICULT BEHAVIOUR – ADVICE

From the Dancer:

> *Where there is difficult behaviour, just talk to them and explain the effect on the team and how it would change their actions. Use a counselling approach at first but eventually you have to dismiss them if there is no change of behaviour.*

From the Banker:

> *Always be fair in how you assess the team members. Be tough on bullying and strive to cut it out. Tackle difficult people early with constructive feedback using empathy, i.e. 'how would you feel?' Ultimately, if they genuinely can't or won't fall into line, push them out by giving them the lowest ratings.*

From the Lead Artist:

> *When a team member behaves badly, talk to the person directly as a first warning. If it happens again, then send them to the office to be talked to by the Office Manager as the second warning. The third time they misbehave they are dropped from the project.*

From the Air Traffic Controller:

> *Do not exclude them but instead include them. Ask them directly for their opinions, particularly in public. Nobody likes to look stupid, so instead of being disruptive they concentrate on giving sensible answers. Also they start to see themselves as having a valid contribution.*
>
> *Confronting them might be necessary but that can put them on the outside where they are always going to be a problem. The last resort should be to warn them that their behaviour could lead to dismissal.*

DEALING WITH DIFFICULT PEOPLE

- ▶ Look for the cause.
- ▶ Deal with performance, not the person.
- ▶ Be descriptive, not evaluative.
- ▶ Don't comment on attitude.
- ▶ Deal with problems while they're small.
- ▶ Don't take sides.

- ► Deal with things in private.
- ► Consider the wider team.
- ► Don't sweep problems under the carpet.
- ► Be prepared to cut your losses.

Finally, here's an interesting point of view on management from Mike Udwin.

Udwin's argument is that no one can 'manage' anyone who doesn't want to be managed, but most management theories encourage you to believe that you can. His solution is to stop trying to manage your people. Instead focus on creating an emotional environment they naturally respond to in a way that embraces good management practice.

He goes on to say:

> *Management isn't something you do to your people. It's something they give you because they want to. This means you have to stop trying to manage people and start to concentrate on leading them instead, leading them in a way that makes them want to be managed by you! That's why some people are easy to manage (because they want to be) and some people are impossible to manage (because they don't want to be!).*

A free copy of Mike Udwin's report **'Why Management Doesn't Work … Until Your Team's Well Led!'** is available from: http://managementdoesntwork.weebly.com/details-page-cd-and-report.html.

KEYS TO A WINNING TEAM

What is leadership?

- Leadership is what you do rather than what you are.
- A leader is someone who can get the job done.

Why is a team leader needed?

- To provide focus and purpose
- To motivate and inspire team members
- Team leaders need followers and vice versa.

What does it take to be a good team leader?

- Have knowledge, skills and confidence so the right things are done right by others.
- Learn how to trust people and how to judge how much to trust other people.

What style of team leadership?

- Autocratic – retains maximum control, members obey orders
- Bureaucratic – leader goes by the book, or defers to authority
- Democratic – invites input, and shared decision-making
- Laissez-faire – is 'hands off', gives as much freedom as possible.

Situational Leadership Theory:

- Team leaders need to be flexible and adapt their style to the situation they are in.

Being assertive and dealing with difficult behaviour:

- When you act assertively, you get what you want or need, without putting down colleagues, while ensuring that their needs and wants are met too.

- Deal with the performance not the person; don't take sides; handle the matter in private and be prepared to cut your losses.

4

How to create a balanced team

In this chapter you will learn:
- *how to identify the personality types within your team*
- *how to place team members in the roles to which they're best suited*
- *about the most commonly used tools for team member profiling.*

Why is a balanced team important?

Do you want a collection of brilliant minds or a brilliant collection of minds?

R. Meredith Belbin

From the RAF Officer:

This is really down to having good Personnel/Human Resource teams who employ people with the correct experience, carry out regular reporting and documenting of an individual's progress within the company and identify training needs for team members to ensure that they have the correct skill sets. From this it is possible when forming teams to obtain information from a central source.

Teams work best when they are carefully balanced and team members possess a range of different skills. You don't want a team full of leaders and no followers. Your team won't get very far either if all your team members are excellent at collaborating with one another, supporting the ideas of their colleagues and working hard to get things done but none of them can think up original ideas. If all your team members have plenty of ideas all the time, but there's no attempt to follow any of these through together, progress will always be limited.

Team leaders have a tendency to recruit members who have similar knowledge, skills and attitudes – 'people like us'. This can sabotage success in a team. What you really need is a team where these three attributes are all perfectly balanced. To do this you need to take three steps:

1 You need to assess the skills of the people in your team using one of the standard models described below.
2 You then need to analyse the results so you understand better everyone's individual capabilities.
3 You then need to apply those results in practice by assigning team members to roles that best match their skills.

Let's look at some practical examples of the skills needed in a specific context before turning to the more general theoretical models. Every team in whatever industry or sector will have a number of different roles that need filling. Here's what the Lead Artist on a community project had to say when she was asked about the roles in her team.

Identify the types within your team

From the Lead Artist:

How important to you is a balanced team and assigning people to the right roles? If so, how do you do it?

First of all, a team leader needs to be interested and compassionate enough to get to know the team members individually. In a project team for a community project you will usually have:

Lead Artist	*the boss – no time to be friends with team*
Assistant artist	*can be a friend to the team as has more time*
Public speaker	*the project's public face*
Hard grafter	*manually dextrous*
Background fillers	*good workers but poor at detail*
Motivators	*jokers – keeping the team's spirits high*
Carriers	*fetching water – cleaning brushes*
Organizers	*keeping track of materials*
Finishers	*good at detailed work*

How do you identify different personality types within the team?

Look, listen and learn in the first few days

From the RAF Officer:

How do you create a balanced team?

By having an awareness of the different personality types and observation of the team. Management courses should include training of this aspect.

Armed with accurate profiles, the team leader is in a much stronger position to assign team members to the right roles.

> **Exercise**
> What are the roles you need to fill in your team?
>
> Take a moment to think about it and then write them down.
> Are they similar in their own way to the project described above?
>
> It would seem that most organizations need their hard grafters, background fillers, motivators organizers and finishers, though they may go by different names.

Next comes a summary of a selection of tools to help you find out just who your team members really are.

Use the available tools to help

Sound theory makes good practice.

Unknown

From the RAF Officer:

I have not used them directly but have been involved in the use of the Myers Briggs tests. Personally, I think that personal knowledge of the person (by an experienced manager) is paramount. Psychometric testing, in my opinion, has its use in giving clues to the personality of new employees.

However, when filling in the forms for such tests, I find it hard to believe that all people give honest answers to the questions.

They want to give a good impression. I am aware that there are devices in the testing to detect inconsistencies but they are not as good as direct observation.

This section provides an outline of four different profiling tools picked because they are widely used and because they have stood the test of time. References are provided where you can obtain more information should you wish to pursue one or other method further. These are products which are generally under licence and a fee is payable to the respective copyright holder for the use of the tool in question, usually a questionnaire followed by some form of analysis.

- ▶ Belbin® (Team Role Theory)
- ▶ MBTI® (Myers-Briggs Type Indicator)
- ▶ SDI® (Strength Deployment Inventory®)
- ▶ *Psycho*-Geometrics® (Shapes)

To help you orientate yourself, here is a brief guide to the differences between the tools.

Belbin is about the team as a whole and identifies the roles that need to be adopted within the team to ensure the team's success.

The other three focus on individual styles of behaviour and how they interact dynamically with the styles of others.

MBTI® is based on the fact that each individual finds certain ways of thinking and acting more comfortable than others. It sorts these preferences into four opposite pairs giving 16 personality type combinations.

SDI® shows what motivates people, not just who they are. It divides people into three colour types. The insight of SDI® is to recognize that people shift their behaviour style when under pressure or when conflict arises.

Psycho-Geometrics'® strength is the simplicity of the concept where people are assigned one of five shapes corresponding to five personality types in terms of lifestyle, ambition, style of dress and surroundings.

For all four models, once you understand your own personality and behaviour style and you have learned to interpret those of your fellow team members, you can adapt your style to each individual to build good relationships, enhance communication and reduce the risk of conflict.

After you have studied these models and gained a flavour of each one, you can select the one that you feel is most appropriate to your situation and your team and try it out. You can even use a combination of models. For example, a team member will understand more about themselves if they go through Belbin profiling and MBTI®. The sum of the two adds up to more than the parts in terms of understanding.

These theories can seem quite complicated at first sight, particularly if you don't have any knowledge of psychology, but actually the theories are surprisingly easy to understand at a basic level. Often the real benefit is to show you how everyone is different. You may not come away being completely familiar with the theories but you will have improved your insight. Team leaders or members who are really interested are encouraged to undertake further reading.

These theories and tools are important if the team wants to gain a real insight into their colleagues.

Whereas Belbin's theory is based on nine types of working style, Myers Briggs is much more about personality type. Myers-Briggs defines four personality types: the brisk 'controller', the sensitive 'feeler', the intelligent 'thinker', and the joke-telling 'entertainer'. People reveal these traits through their tone or their choice of words, and others modify their conversation to fit.

None is better or worse than the other and each is different; they just have different applications. Sometimes people are given a full set of tests and will have a variety of profiles where the findings complement each other.

BELBIN® TEAM ROLE THEORY

One of the most common team-building theories is that of Dr Meredith Belbin. In the 1970s and 80s Belbin devised a questionnaire which illustrated the different behaviours of workers. Belbin's *Management Teams–Why They Succeed Or Fail*, (Butterworth-Heinemann, 2010) presented conclusions from his work studying how members of teams interacted during business games run at Henley Management College. One of his key conclusions was that an effective team has members that cover eight (later nine) key roles in managing the team and how it carries out its work.

An example of a Belbin type is a Resource Investigator, one who is extrovert, enthusiastic, communicative, explores opportunities and develops contacts. Importantly, the Belbin theory gives each type 'allowable weaknesses'. In the case of the Resource Investigator these weaknesses are that they can be over optimistic and lose interest once initial enthusiasm has passed.

This is very important, as one of the key features of a successful team is that each member understands their colleagues and takes account of their strengths and weaknesses. So, for example, if someone is always letting you down for the same reason, then stop depending on them for that thing.

Practical implications

Based on Belbin's model of nine team roles (see following pages), as a team leader choosing your team, you would be well advised to make sure that each of the roles can be performed by one of your team members. Some roles are compatible and can be more easily fulfilled by the same person; some are less compatible and are likely to be done well by people with different behavioural characteristics. This means that a team need not be as many as nine people but perhaps should be at least three or four.

How to use

To find out which of the nine Belbin® Team Roles you and your team members have an affinity towards and which ones you don't, you need to start by completing a Belbin Self-Perception Inventory. This is a questionnaire that takes about 20 minutes to complete. Your scores are interpreted by Belbin's e-interplace® programme. Your report is generated and sent back to you within minutes.

For more information go to: www.belbin.com

The copyright for the Belbin® Team Role Theory model and materials is held by:

Belbin Associates, 3-4 Bennell Court, West Street, Comberton, Cambridge CB23 7EN, tel: 01223 264975

Belbin's team role theory

Key role	Definition	Benefit
Plant:	A creative, imaginative, unorthodox team member who solves difficult problems.	Although they sometimes situate themselves far from the other team members, they always come back to present their 'brilliant' idea.
Resource Investigator:	The networker for the group. Whatever the team needs, the Resource Investigator is likely to know someone who can provide it or know someone else who can.	Being highly driven to make connections with people, the Resource Investigator may appear to be flighty and inconstant, but their ability to call on their connections is highly useful to the team.
Chairman (1981) / Co-ordinator (1988):	The one who ensures that all members of the team are able to contribute to discussions and decisions of the team. Their concern is for fairness and equity among team members.	Those who want to make decisions quickly, or unilaterally, may feel frustrated by their insistence on consulting with all members, but this can often improve the quality of decisions made by the team.

Shaper:	A dynamic team member who loves a challenge and thrives on pressure.	Possesses the drive and courage required to overcome obstacles.
Monitor Evaluator:	A sober, strategic and discerning member, who tries to see all options and judge accurately.	Contributes a measured and dispassionate analysis and stops the team committing itself to a misguided task.
Teamworker:	A conciliator concerned that interpersonal relationships are maintained. Their sensitivity means they may be first to approach a member who feels slighted or excluded but has not expressed their discomfort.	Concern with people factors can frustrate those who are keen to move quickly, but their skills ensure long-term cohesion within the team.
Company Worker (1981) / Implementer (1988):	The practical thinker who can create systems and processes that will produce what the team wants. Their strength is taking a problem and working out how it can be practically addressed.	Strongly rooted in the real world, they may frustrate others by their perceived lack of enthusiasm for inspiring visions and radical thinking, but their ability to turn those ideas into workable solutions is important.

Belbin's team role theory

Key role	Definition	Benefit
Completer Finisher:	Acting as the detail person within the team, they have a great eye for spotting flaws and gaps and for knowing exactly where the team is in relation to its schedule.	Those with less preference for detailed work may be frustrated by their analytical and meticulous approach but their work ensures the quality and timeliness of the team's output.
Specialist (1988):	Belbin later added a ninth role, the 'Specialist' who brings specialist knowledge to the team.	Passionate about learning in their own particular field, they strive to improve and build upon their expertise. However, they can only contribute that specialism by being uninterested in anything outside its narrow confines.

Adapted from Belbin, Dr R Meredith, *Management Teams–Why They Succeed Or Fail* (Butterworth-Heinemann, 2010).

MYERS-BRIGGS TYPE INDICATOR (MBTI®)

Now for the second powerful and popular profile tool – the Myers-Briggs Type Indicator or MBTI® for short. MBTI® is a personality questionnaire designed to identify certain psychological differences. The original developers of the indicator were Katharine Cook Briggs and her daughter, Isabel Briggs Myers. They began developing the indicator during World War II.

The MBTI® is based on Jung's concept in his book *Psychological Types*. Just like being left- or right-handed, people find some ways of acting and thinking easier than others. The MBTI sorts some of these psychological characteristics into four opposite pairs – or *dichotomies*. These are:

▶ Extrovert to Introvert (E to I)
▶ Sensation to Intuition (S to N)
▶ Thinking to Feeling (T to F)
▶ Judging to Perceiving (J to P).

These four opposite pairs can be combined into 16 unique combinations. None is 'right' or 'wrong' or in any sense 'better' or 'worse' but Myers and Briggs understood that people have a preferred combination that suits them best. Using the opposite indicator, if not impossible, is difficult. Trying to be an introvert when your preferred tendency is extrovert is hard. It's like trying to write left-handed when you are right-handed. However, people can learn to be more proficient and flexible with practise and development.

The preferences are normally indicated by the first letters of each of their four preferences. So for instance:

▶ **ISTJ** – Introverted, Sensing, Thinking, Judging
▶ **ENFP** – Extroverted, Intuitive, Feeling, Perceiving.

and so on for all 16 possible combinations.

On completing the MBTI®, a team member will end up with a score between the two polar extremes that will define their preference. For example, a person will have a tendency to be either an Extrovert or an Introvert but they cannot be both. At the end of the survey each team member will have a profile, for example, this might be ESTJ (Extroverted, Sensing, Thinking, Judging).

The objective of experiencing the MBTI® in this context is to increase understanding of yourself and others in your team as well as prompting you to value the differences between you. The following are pointers to the behaviours associated with the four Myers Briggs functions, as relevant to team building and communication. This is a brief summary of the MBTI® functions. There is a wealth of information on this subject available in book form and online. To find out more, see the references at the end of this section.

These short descriptions give an overview of what MBTI® is about:

Extroverts and Introverts
Extroverts ('Es'): do not know what they are thinking until they say it. They may change direction as they speak, as things become clearer as they go along.

Introverts ('Is'): need to think things through. They become uneasy if discussion is thrust on them as they need to go away to consider.

Sensors and Intuitives
Sensors ('Ss'): use specifics such as facts, dates and times. They are irritated by vagueness. Problem definition is important.

Intuitives ('Ns'): see specifics as limiting and look at the big picture. They may agree with specific details presented by an 'S' but can only understand the 'whole'.

Thinkers and Feelers
Thinkers ('Ts'): will set their emotions to one side so their feelings will not enter into the logical analysis of a situation. They will not make an immediate decision, preferring to step back to analyse the facts.

Feelers ('Fs'): are 'people people' and judge situations on a personal level, taking into account personal values. They are often torn because they are able to see both sides of any situation.

Judgers and Perceivers
Judgers ('Js'): favour exactness and want to know how long things will take. They will make an appointment for 4.30 and arrive at 4.29.

Perceivers ('Ps'): will put off the final decision for as long as possible. They favour tolerance and open time-frames.

Interpretation

Remember that the interaction between these four opposites makes up the 16 possible combinations, i.e. ESTJ, INFP, ESFP, etc.

People vary in the degree to which they polarize towards these preferences. For some the influence is weak but in others it is strong enough to affect the whole way they approach their life. The MBTI® shows this and helps people to understand themselves and the others within their team.

This useful tool can be linked to building a balanced team. As team members learn about their MBTI® profiles and experience these through their daily interactions with their colleagues, they can learn how to handle interpersonal situations with more insight. Over time this will create a more harmonious and less stressful teamwork environment.

How to use

To administer an MBTI® test, you first need to take a qualifying course run by OPP. You are then able to purchase and deliver the MBTI® questionnaire and analyse the results. See www.opp.eu.com.

MBTI in action

Tom Lamont in the Guardian Online (Dec 2010) describes a visit to a call centre whose agents had been taught MBTI® to improve their communication skills with their customers by recognizing their MBTI® personality types and adapting their manner accordingly. According to John Connolly, head of innovation at British Gas, customers reveal these traits through their tone or their choice of words and agents modify their conversation to fit: 'If a thinker wants to chat about taking a trip to Legoland you chat about Legoland. You wouldn't ask a controller [judger] what they're doing at the weekend.'

Guardian, 19 December 2010 http://www.guardian.co.uk/business/2010/dec/19/call-centres-makeover-alan-sugar

Myers-Briggs Type Indicator, MBTI, and Myers-Briggs are trademarks or registered trademarks of the MBTI Trust, Inc.

OPP Ltd is licensed to use the trade marks in Europe. Contact OPP at: Elsfield Hall, 15–17 Elsfield Way, Oxford OX2 8EP United Kingdom; Tel: +44 (0)845 603 9958; Email: enquiry@opp.eu.com; Website: www.opp.eu.com.

> ### Exercise
> ▶ Which Myers-Briggs type are you?
> ▶ Do you recognize yourself here in any of the types described?
> ▶ Or are you a mixture of types?

STRENGTH DEPLOYMENT INVENTORY® (SDI®)

Another useful management tool is the Strength Deployment Inventory® (SDI®). SDI® will show you what motivates you and what motivates other people. Companies offering SDI® say that it enables everyone to understand the reason why people do things, rather than just observe and react to what is done. This can be extremely useful for a team leader.

SDI® is very easy to use and divides people into three colours:

▶ Red types are aggressive, goal orientated and prone to very direct communication.
▶ Blue types are relationship focused and more gentle and social.
▶ Green types are the detailed type; they understand how things work and like data.

SDI® shows how Reds can upset other types, Blues can seem too nice and poor old Greens can be viewed as boring. Interestingly, SDI® shows that many people change type when under pressure. For example, someone who becomes a Blue under pressure can feel tearful if they are not used to that state and those who become extremely Red should be avoided.

This is a useful tool as it is easy to understand and team members quickly gain a greater understanding, not only of the motivation of their own team but of their family, friends and almost everyone they meet.

To meet their needs for self-esteem and self-worth, people all behave in a way with which they feel comfortable. Some feel rewarded by being logical and analytical, others by achieving goals and still more by helping others. When they interact with other people within this 'comfort zone' their experience of their relationships gives rise to feelings of self-worth and self-esteem. SDI helps you to understand this process and use it to deepen your understanding of the people around you.

Look at the following analogy concerning an ambulance and how it is driven. It shows how judging behaviour on its own may be misleading.

> *On the way to an accident the ambulance is driven fast, breaking speed limits and passing through red lights, even driving on the hard shoulder. On its way from the accident to the hospital however, it is driven slowly, with caution and with care for the injured patient. So two very different patterns of behaviour, but the motivation behind them is the same which is the welfare of others. Being recognized for providing this welfare for others provides a sense of self-esteem and self-worth for those with a blue or nurturing MVS [motivational value systems].*

Howard Rose, Inspire Development Ltd

Who developed the SDI®?

SDI® was developed by Dr Elias H. Porter who worked alongside Carl Rogers, originator of client centred therapy. During his time studying at the University of California, Porter developed 'Relationship Awareness Theory' which states that motivation is the basis of all behaviour and you need to feel a sense of self-worth and self-esteem in your relationships with others.

Dr Porter devised a questionnaire so you can understand what really motivates you to behave as you do. When the questions are answered truthfully, they offer insight into your true motivations.

SDI® provides a unique understanding about relationships. First, people fill in their own motivational styles profile. Following this they start to examine how this relates to the actual behaviour they choose in a given situation.

Each individual SDI® profile is created by filling out a short inventory that asks about two conditions: how you deploy your strengths when things are going well and also when you face conflict.

SDI® uses three colours – blue, red and green. With their blends (red-blue, red-green, blue-green and red-blue-green (known as 'hub')) this represents the **seven motivational value systems** (MVS) outlined below. This makes SDI® easy to complete and remember. These motivational value systems expand into over a million individual positions where none is any better than any other.

Altruistic-Nurturing (blue)	The protection, growth and welfare of others. Looking for opportunities to support those who may need help.
Assertive-Directing (red)	Task accomplishment, organization of people, time and money plus any other resources... to win out against opposition and be seen as an achiever.
Analytical-Autonomizing (green)	The assurance that things have been properly thought out, self-dependence, taking time to get things 'right', looking for ways to improve quality.
Flexible-Cohering (hub)	Flexibility, the welfare of the group and for belonging in the group. Keeping options open, consensus and harmony within groups.
Assertive-Nurturing (red-blue)	The protection, growth and welfare of others through task accomplishment and leadership. Enthusiasm for the development of others.
Judicious-Competing (red-green)	Intelligent assertiveness, justice, order and fairness in competition. Strategic thinking where all resources are used to achieve goals.
Cautious-Supporting (blue-green)	Affirming and developing self-sufficiency in self and others. Concern for thoughtful helpfulness with regard to justice.

What happens when conflict occurs?

While conflict between people can never be completely avoided, teams that understand each other's value systems greatly reduce the chances of conflict happening. When it does, SDI® gives you insights not only into why people change their styles, but how to recognize the shifts early and how to resolve potential conflict quickly and appropriately.

Much conflict is unnecessary and the costs of conflict to the individual and to the organization include slow and poor decision-making, time lost, stress, poor morale and lower profits. Being aware of your own and others' MVS can substantially reduce this type of conflict, research shows.

How can it help you?
So how can SDI® help you and your organization?

> **Exercise**
> Can you think of a single role in your organization that is completely autonomous or that requires no interaction with others, i.e. one that has no information, no discussion and no support? Did you find it hard, perhaps impossible?

That's because all individuals interact with other people. As organizations are constantly required to do more with less, you find yourself working more and more closely with others, at a variety of complex levels. In today's businesses conflict can damage your personal and organizational productivity more than ever before.

A key element in the understanding of others is to develop high self-awareness first. SDI® allows you to increase your personal understanding. With this fresh look at yourself and others and the acceptance that everyone is different, you become more tolerant of others' ideas and solutions to problems. This awareness helps you spot the early signals of tension between people that leads to unnecessary conflict.

When you develop this new awareness, you can avoid the conflict escalating into those full-blown arguments you have probably seen or experienced. You are then able to develop new ways of working with those who you see as different to yourself. You are able to develop ways to be more productive with others and this will lead to greater harmony, more commitment from the team and less personal stress – all of which should lead to improved performance.

Where can SDI® be used?

SDI® can be used in any situation where people interact with other people. One area where SDI® would be valuable is that of team building, especially newly formed teams or teams who are in conflict and not working together productively. In this case the members learn to fully appreciate what it is that drives their colleagues to seek reward and are also far more aware of the early stages of conflict between team members. SDI® equips us to deal with these situations earlier and more effectively, leading to greater team harmony and productivity.

The second area would be in a role where influencing is a key factor, such as sales or leadership. Understanding the four Motivational Value Systems (MVS) and identifying them in your client or subordinate will give you the information required to communicate and offer them feedback as individuals in a way they find rewarding, thus strengthening the relationship providing greater trust and co-operation.

Howard Rose, Director Inspire Development Ltd,
www.inspiredevelopment.co.uk

How to use

SDI® is administered in the UK by Personal Strengths UK. Like many companies that publish and market assessment tools, they have a certification process. In order to purchase and facilitate SDI® tools, you need to become qualified by attending one of their workshops offered throughout the world.

You can contact **Personal Strengths UK at The Old School, 60 Queen Street, Stamford, Lincs. PE9 1QS; Tel: 01780 480102**; Website: http://uk.personalstrengths.com or at www.personalstrengths.com if outside the UK.

Exercise
► Which SDI® colour type are you?
► Do you recognize yourself in any of the descriptions?
► Or are you a mixture of types?

PSYCHO-GEOMETRICS®

Our final model is the *Psycho*-Geometrics® system which was developed by Dr Susan E. Dellinger in 1978. The key idea here is that every personality can be defined by a shape. This system looks at behaviour from the perspective that:

> *... people come in all sizes but there are only five personality shapes.*
>
> Dr Susan Dellinger

Each shape describes a personality in terms of lifestyle, ambition, style of dress and surroundings. To start with *Psycho*-Geometrics® you first choose a shape you feel that defines your personality from any one of the five in Figure 4.1:

From these personality types, people can discover more about themselves, their attitudes and the people with whom they come in

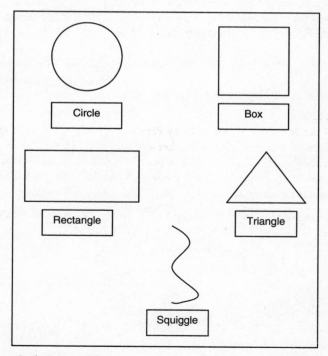

Figure. 4.1 Psycho-Geometrics® shapes.

contact. They can learn how to improve difficult personal conflicts and build healthy colleague, client and customer relationships.

The system has been used to good effect as a large team exercise consisting of four steps:

▶ Step 1: Ask each person to draw the five shapes.
▶ Step 2: Ask them to number them in their order of preference from 1 to 5.
▶ Step 3: Ask them to find other people in the room who match their first two shape preferences.
▶ Step 4: Explain and interpret the significance of the five shapes.

This goes along the following lines:

Box	Perfectionist; always does homework	Colleagues come to you for help.
Circle	'Touchy-feely'	People bring you their personal problems.
Rectangle	Entertainer; shape shifter	You are always the last to know.
Squiggle	'Nutter'; unpredictable	You often embarrass your friends.
Triangle	Leader; reach for the top	You always get the best deals; you get the job done.

You can try the Shape Analysis method on your colleagues. Ask them to choose one of the shapes and then take a look at their behaviour and even their work area to see if they were accurate!

When you use the insights gained from Shape Analysis to look at how your team members behave, you will see ways to improve your working relationships. In so doing you will help to make your team more productive and more effective. Having an insight into why people behave in certain ways should help you and your team members become more tolerant of each other's working habits.

If you wish to discover what shape you really are, you can complete the free online questionnaire at www.psychometricshapes.co.uk/questionnaire.php. Once you have completed this process you can explore the attributes of all the shapes and combination of shapes.

Here is a short summary of each of the profiles belonging to the five shapes:

- ▶ The **circle person** is a creature of comfort. Circles are very much focused on the wellbeing of others and on maintaining harmony. They do not cope well with conflict and will often back down in the face of an argument. In general, Circles are good communicators who can listen and empathize well with others.
- ▶ The **box person** (or Square), is the most organized of the shapes. They are the most knowledgeable and are dependable and patient. Obsessional and perfectionist, the box person is often viewed as a loner and is most definitely not a team player.
- ▶ The **rectangle person** is disorganized and incredibly messy – their desks are swamped with piles of stuff. Their lack of focus and a great deal of indecision and inconsistency mean that there are almost always several items waiting to be properly filed away.
- ▶ The **squiggle person** is far from tidy. These individuals tend to be exceptionally creative, flamboyant, dramatic, and witty and are the messiest and least organized of all the shapes. They can however be very motivating people to be around.
- ▶ The **triangle person**, like the box person, is very organized although maybe not to quite the same extent. They are very focused. The desk of a triangle person is likely to be relatively clear with a few distinct piles of work placed upon it. It is most definitely not cluttered.

Acknowledgements to Dr Dellinger's website at
www.psychometricshapes.co.uk

Communicating with each shape

Susan Hite, a *Psycho*-Geometrics® practitioner, gives a good account of how best to behave with each shape type.

BOX
- ▶ Be calm and in control. Be professional, without pressure but ask for results based on facts (no emotion).
- ▶ Use details, figures, dates, times and names in your interaction. Boxes like agendas and time to prepare and process information.

TRIANGLE
- Be assertive and think bottom line.
- Show respect first but also demonstrate your own level of competence. Less is best.
- Offer two or three options, if possible, based on your research prior to talking to the triangle.

RECTANGLE
- Be open minded and prepared to answer numerous questions.
- After listening, be firm about direction and choices, set a time limit for your interaction or 'test-run' of a new idea/ project.

CIRCLE
- Be warm, friendly and chatty but explain time limitations up front.
- 'Circles don't care how much you know, until they know how much you care.'
- Relationships are key.

SQUIGGLE
- Be enthusiastic, while staying focused on the subject at hand.
- Explain the unique features of the product/service/project and/or be willing to explain **why** and what's in it for them; be firm on options/consequences.
- Allow room for creativity.

Adapted from Hite, S. (2005) *Ignite*, www.susanhite.com/subscription_content/E-IgniteAug05.pdf

How to use
Psycho-Geometrics® LLC owns all presentation and distribution rights. You need to become licensed and pay a one-off fee before you may deliver the questionnaire, though it is available for individuals to take online.

Contact: *Psycho*-**Geometrics**® LLC, 5701 Mariner St., Suite 601, Tampa, FL 33609; Tel: +1 800-762-3478; Email: info@ psychogeometrics.com; Website: www.psychometricshapes.co.uk

Now you've had the chance to review four different models of personality profiling.

Insight

Bearing in mind they each do different things, overall they address a common issue. This answers the question: 'What type of people do I have in my team?' Knowing that, the follow up question is 'how can I use these insights to best effect and run a team that is both efficient and harmonious?'

Assign people to the right roles

The more you understand the characteristics, personalities and motivators of your team members, the better position you are in to put them into the right roles and the team will function much better as a result.

> *Be sensitive to the skills and interests of your employees as you assign them to jobs. Try to put people in jobs that suit them. Put the dreamer in charge of creative tasks. Put the detail-oriented individual on tasks with more structure. Don't put your introverted loner into customer service. Just think how much more would get done if people only did jobs for which they had the talent, and a real passion.*

F. John Reh, About.com Guide

SO WHAT DO YOU DO?

The licences for questionnaires and analysis are subject to copyright and have a cost attached. Where you intend to use them a great deal, someone in your team can train to become a qualified practitioner and deliver them across the organization.

Beware of using unlicensed or illegally copied psychometrics instruments and check that any tools that are apparently free and in the public domain are actually so. The tools described here should not be used without a licence or the officially purchased materials from the relevant providers.

WHICH ONE SHOULD YOU USE FOR WHICH PURPOSE?

The short answer is:

- ▶ Belbin® when you are building a team
- ▶ MBTI® when you want to find out what people are like
- ▶ SDI® when you want to find out what makes your people tick
- ▶ *Psycho*-Geometrics® when you want a personal profile.

Or indeed, a combination of Belbin® plus one other to give a more rounded picture of your people.

Remember that people are more motivated when performing in a way that comes naturally to them. To expect someone with a particular personality type (whether it is represented by a Belbin® team role, MBTI®, SDI® or whatever) to perform well in a role that does not suit their natural preferences or play to their strengths is not helpful.

WHY IS IT IMPORTANT TO UNDERSTAND PERSONALITY PROFILING?

As you can see, all four models aim at the same goal – that of helping you and your team members better understand each other's behaviour so you can have a balanced team that works together efficiently and effectively. They have much in common.

Different people respond to different stimuli and the more you understand each other, the more you see what motivates your team members. The more you understand about your own personality and that of other people, the better able you are to realize how others perceive you and how they react to your own personality and style.

The main factors that will help you successfully manage and motivate others – and yourself – are knowing how you:

- ▶ adapt the way you work with others
- ▶ access information and learning opportunities
- ▶ identify and agree tasks.

While it is useful to use psychometric tools, the long-standing benefit comes from working with these models to understand the logic and theory underpinning the personality models concerned. Each theory helps you to understand more about yourself and others.

By studying the content provided here you will not become a qualified trainer. However, you should acquire enough information from one or more models to apply to your own behaviour and that of your team's, and gain fresh insights into your team members' characters and behaviours.

Where you have the opportunity to build a new team from scratch and select your team members, then it will help you have the knowledge and the confidence to select the right people and it will have served its purpose by showing you how to create a balanced team.

You have seen four personality models here. They have been selected as among the best known and most widely used. There are many other models including, for example, Benzinger's Brain Type Theory, Eysenck's Personality Types Theory, Marston's DISC Personality Theory and the Big Five Factors Personality Model. Do feel free to explore wider and deeper.

Exercise
▶ Think about the four models.
▶ Which do you think would be most useful to you?
▶ Consider taking the one of your choice further by making the investment to get the team to take the questionnaires and have them analysed.

KEYS TO A WINNING TEAM

Why is a balanced team important?

- Knowing the different personality types of your team members and the role that suits them best is a very powerful tool.

Identify types within the team:

- Identify the roles that need filling in your team.

Use the available tools to help:

- All the tools described are solutions that help you gain a deeper understanding of your team and how you and they interact.

- Belbin® Team Role Theory defines nine key roles to describe how a team carries out its work.

- Myers-Briggs (MBTI®) identifies an individual's preferences for Extroversion or Introversion, Sensing or Intuition, Thinking or Feeling, Judging or Perceiving.

- SDI® (Strength Deployment Inventory®) is based on Porter's theory of Relationship Awareness and uses colours for its analysis.

- *Psycho*-Geometrics® uses five shapes to describe different personality types.

- Choose and use the technique that suits your team best.

- The tools described above should not be used without a licence or the officially purchased materials from the relevant providers.

Assign people to the right roles:

- You can create a balanced team by assigning team members to roles that match their personality profiles.

5

How to work as a team

In this chapter you will learn:
- *about different types of teams*
- *what type of team you are in*
- *how teams develop.*

What team are you in?

From the Air Traffic Controller:

I have worked with both [new and existing teams]. New teams, in particular, require careful handling. Because you are in uncharted waters and the objectives are still being developed, some team members might tend to go off in their own direction. Sometimes this is good because they might find good ways to do things but it has to be carefully monitored.

Are you inheriting an existing team or do you have the opportunity to start a new team? Different types of team exist to serve a variety of different purposes. For example, is your team interdependent or independent, a project team or an inter- or multidisciplinary team? It's helpful to understand the type of team you're in.

Sometimes your team members won't be sharing the same physical location as you, existing as a virtual team nationally or even globally. With the coming of the internet and fast broadband capability, such teams are becoming more common. Is leading a virtual team different? What considerations should you bear in mind?

Another type of team is one without a team leader, usually referred to as a self-managed team. Is this possible and how do they work? Are they really leaderless and under what conditions do they flourish?

Teams take time to grow together and they go through stages of development. This process has been mapped both by George O. Charrier's 'Cog's Ladder' (1972) and Bruce Tuckman's model of 'Storming, Forming, Norming, Performing' (1965). Both models are described later in this chapter so you can understand better how teams develop.

There's a tendency for team members to think in different ways and in different modes. One person may be thinking rationally, one emotionally, another optimistically, while someone else is being pessimistic. Edward de Bono's *Six Thinking Hats* (Viking, 1985) helps teams think together more effectively and plan their thinking in a more detailed and cohesive way. With its metaphor of six coloured hats, it provides an easy to remember model and useful tool for efficient decision-making.

Exercise

▶ Ask yourself what type of team you are in.
▶ Find the answers in the material that follows. It will help you understand exactly that.

When the team is new:

▶ it's an opportunity, especially if you get to choose your own team members
▶ it's also a challenge to start from scratch, as teams take time to develop
▶ you need to consider what conditions you should set, or whether the team itself should decide.

On the other hand, when you inherit an existing team:

▶ there's less scope for matching personalities to roles
▶ you may have been appointed from within the team or been brought in from outside.

In either case and in different ways, it's a real challenge to win the trust, respect and confidence of your new or existing team members.

From the Project Director:

What are the challenges of working with an existing teams?

The organization comprises an existing team of seven people with entrenched relationships and often negative attitudes. An example is the Finance Director who was not doing the job properly. This affected other people by using up their time asking for unnecessary statistics and holding unfocused, unstructured meetings.

Here are some good common sense tips adapted from James Citrin and Thomas Neff, *You're in Charge, Now What?* (Three Rivers Press, 2007):

1 Prepare before you start the job
2 Under promise and over deliver
3 Pick and brief your team
4 Determine your strategic focus
5 Communicate what you are doing
6 Avoid making common mistakes.

In essence this can be reduced to 'listen and learn'.

Citrin and Neff focus on the importance of making an impact during your first one hundred days and quote Lawrence Summers, former president of Harvard University who:

... failed to appreciate that if you're going to be questioning everybody and challenging everybody, you have to do a lot of reassuring in return.

Exercise
Ask yourself:

▶ Is your team a new team or an existing one?
▶ What special challenges do you face?
▶ Take a moment to consider how you will deal with them.

DIFFERENT TYPES OF TEAMS

Not all teams are the same and some teams may not even be teams at all. Look at these different types of teams:

▶ interdependent teams vs independent teams
▶ project teams
▶ interdisciplinary and multidisciplinary teams.

Interdependent teams vs independent teams

A football team is an example of an interdependent team:

- ► Successful play requires co-operation between team members.
- ► Within the team, members typically specialize in different tasks (goal keeping, defending, attacking, goal scoring).
- ► The success of each individual is connected to the success of the whole team.
- ► No footballer, no matter how talented, has ever won a game by playing alone.

A chess team is an example of an independent team:

- ► Here the team is really a collection of brilliant individuals.
- ► Matches are played and won by individuals.
- ► Every player performs basically similar actions.
- ► Whether one player wins or loses has no direct effect on the performance of the next player.
- ► By analogy, if all the team's members perform the same basic tasks, such as sales staff making calls, then this team is more than likely to be an independent team.

In the example of sales staff, each sales person's success is generally achieved through their own efforts. While they may help each other out or give advice from time to time, ultimately they belong to an independent team working on their own. Similarly, chess players do not win their matches because the rest of their team members did.

'Interdependent' and 'independent' teams are clearly very different and need to be led in a style that is appropriate to their nature.

Interdependent teams	*Independent teams*
► Benefit from getting to know the other team members socially	► See no benefit in social activities; considered as emotional time wasters
► Benefit from developing trust in each other	► Benefit from more intellectual, job related training
► Create opportunities for the team to socialize outside the office Consider a team-building event to build trust between members	► To improve the team's performance often the best way is a single question, 'What does everyone need to do a better job?'

Project teams

A project team tends to be a team used for a defined period of time and for a separate, clearly defined purpose. The project team is defined by having a common function and its members might belong to other groups being assigned to this project for its limited duration before they return to their regular role. Additionally the project team may not be full time, meeting weekly or monthly as required.

Sometimes a project team is not a real team at all. Assigning a group of people based on a project in hand does not necessarily mean those people are actually working as a team.

A project team leader's role may be temporary, appointed solely for the project's duration or a more permanent one where he/she is always a project team leader, moving from project to project.

Because a project is, by definition, limited in time span, the emphasis will tend to be more on meeting the project's objective and getting the task done than on the people or social side, though that remains important too. The team's task is simply stated, if harder to fulfil. It is to deliver the project on time, on budget and to quality.

To be a professional and effective project team leader who delivers, you need to be competent in the following skills:

► *Strategic vision* – Oversee the daily development of individual components; coordinate their deadlines, leading to a successful delivery of the final project.

► *Troubleshooting* – Make immediate decisions to troubleshoot issues that arise as the project progresses. Act as mediator among team members to resolve conflicts promptly.

► *Communication* – Coordinate meetings with clients, staff, contractors and company managers. Act as a point person for immediate status updates or when changes must be communicated to the team.

► *Quality assurance* – Be responsible for the project's end quality. When the team leader is made responsible for quality, the performance of the whole team will often improve because everyone feels accountable.

Interdisciplinary and multidisciplinary teams

Multidisciplinary teams, for example in a medical context, involve several professionals who independently treat various issues a patient may have, focusing on the ones in which they specialize. The problems that are being treated may or may not relate to other issues being addressed by individual team members.

The interdisciplinary team approach involves all members of the team working together towards the same goal. In an interdisciplinary team approach, roles may be swapped by members of the core team who may take on tasks usually filled by other team members.

The nice thing about teamwork is that you always have others on your side.

Margaret Carty

Exercise

Take a moment to consider which type of team you are in:

▶ Are you in an interdependent or independent team?
▶ Is your team a project team with a limited time span or a more permanent team?
▶ Do you have team members from different disciplines or do you all share a common background?

How well do virtual teams and self-managed teams work?

SELF-MANAGED TEAMS

My role in society, or any artist's or poet's role, is to try and express what you all feel. Not to tell people how to feel. Not as a preacher, not as a leader but as a reflection of us all.

John Lennon

People want to listen to a message... This could be passed through me or anybody. I am not a leader. I am a messenger. The words of the songs, not the person, is what attracts people.

Bob Marley

There's an irony in both these quotes from these great – and sadly late – figures in popular culture. They both claim not to be leaders and that their role is to be the messenger through whom the meaning passes. And yet, in spite of what they say, they were both regarded very much as leaders for their generation by many young people both during their lives and that reputation has lasted and even grown to this day.

'Leaderless' self-managed teams share something of the same ambiguity. They should exist without leaders. Different team members should emerge to take the lead at different times. Yet they do seem to need a leader sometimes, especially in their formation. In this type of team, members need coaching and an intensive level of training. While self-managed teams may be possible in theory, how well do they work in practice? What does the evidence show?

What is a self-managed team?
According to *The Business Dictionary* a self-managed team is:

> *a self-organized semi-autonomous small group whose members determine, plan and manage their day-to-day activities and duties in addition to providing other supportive functions under reduced or no supervision.*
>
> www.businessdictionary.com/definition/self-managed-team.html

In a regular team, as opposed to a group, members tend to become more motivated, develop new ideas to improve team performance and take on more responsibility in putting plans into action. A self-managed team is a specific type of team that sustains a high degree of collaboration and that manages itself with the aim of growing into a very high performing team. In self-managed teams, trust grows among the team members as work progresses and they become motivated to accept more difficult challenges. The focus in these types of teams is on performance as well as on teamwork. Their success requires strong personal and company commitment, skills development and support from both fellow team members and management.

Preparation
Self-managed teams do not happen by accident and team members need training to prepare them to work in this new way. People should not be thrown into a self-managed team without proper preparation.

This results in disarray and disorder. The best time for training is when the team is being formed, and then as and when necessary if the team meets situations it cannot handle.

One of the objectives of a self-managed team is that team members are flexible enough to solve unexpected problems as they happen, since no amount of training can prepare people to deal with specific unforeseen problems as they arise.

Self-managed teams still need an adviser

By definition, self-managed teams do not have a team leader but they often have one while on their way to becoming a self-managed team. In addition there is often a need for an adviser or coach whose role is to guide team members and help them improve their decision-making skills through experience. Here the responsibility shifts: from the traditional role of the team leader in getting work done, towards developing the capabilities of the team members. This is done by encouraging discussions, asking questions and providing explanations to raise the team's level of thinking.

Self-managed teams go under different names

Self-managed teams sometimes go under different names, and methodologies such as Agile or SCRUM. Whatever the name, the self-managed team concept remains sound and valid. To perform well, these types of teams need considerable training and coaching. They are hard to get started but, once they are up and running, they are very effective.

VIRTUAL TEAMS

What is a virtual team?

In addition to being a team, the members of virtual teams are separated by time and/or space. Their primary form of interaction is electronic, though they may meet face-to-face occasionally.

The reasons for virtual teams centre on the differences in location and time zone for team members. Specifically, teams may be distributed because of the new realities facing organizations such as geographical location, cost reduction or change in working patterns.

Today, when organizations are more distributed across locations and across industries, they have discovered the value of collaborative work with a new emphasis on knowledge management. Harvesting the experience of members of the organization, wherever that knowledge is located, means it is available to the whole organization. All these developments have changed the way teams are formed and how they operate. Teams have changed from traditional teams to virtual teams in the following ways:

Traditional team	Virtual team
Fixed team membership; all team members drawn from within the organization.	Shifting team membership team members can include people from outside the organization (clients, collaborators).
Team members are dedicated 100 per cent to the team.	Most people are members of multiple teams.
Team members are co-located organizationally and geographically.	Team members are distributed organizationally and geographically.
Teams have a fixed starting and ending point.	Teams form and reform continuously.
Teams are managed by a single manager.	Teams have multiple reporting relationships with different parts of the organization at different times.

Virtual teams enable teamwork

Virtual teams are a great way to enable teamwork where people are not sitting in the same physical office at the same time. Such teams are used more and more by companies and other organizations to cut travel, relocation, office premises and other business costs. Virtual teams are common with organizations that wish to operate on a global scale and need the special skills of their people who don't want to travel or relocate to a new work place.

www.time-management-guide.com

There is one big difference between virtual teams and traditional teams, and that's the way they communicate. Virtual team members lack the opportunity for face-to-face conversations and have to rely on electronic channels such as e-mails, IM (Instant Messaging), phone calls, video-conferencing and virtual meetings.

Due to these communication limitations, not every type of project is suitable for a virtual team. Examples are where a high volume of information is exchanged in real time or where tasks needed to be handed sequentially within a short time from one team member to another.

Not everyone performs well in a virtual team environment. The essential skills are:

▶ being self motivated, able to work on your own without much supervision
▶ being results-driven since no one is there to check on your output
▶ being a good communicator, able to come across clearly, constructively and positively, digitally without non-verbal cues.

Virtual team leaders need to communicate clear rules for goals and performance. It's important to avoid people making their own assumptions. Team members need to know what to expect from each other, so imprecise assumptions need to give way to rules and protocols. In a virtual team, everything has to be tied down much tighter so everyone operates to a common standard.

Building and maintaining trust between team members is even more important in a virtual team than a traditional one. Without trust, people cannot communicate openly and honestly and the team will become demotivated. This needs special attention at every stage of the team's development.

Benefits of virtual teams

Here are some tips for virtual teams from David Gould of Seanet.com:

▶ People can work from anywhere at any time.
▶ People can be recruited for their competencies, not just physical location.
▶ Many physical handicaps are not a problem.
▶ Expenses for travel, accommodation, parking plus leasing or owning a building may be reduced and sometimes eliminated.
▶ There is no commute time.

Tips for virtual team leaders

- ▶ Hold an initial face-to-face start up.
- ▶ Have periodic face-to-face meetings, especially to resolve conflict and maintain team cohesiveness.
- ▶ Establish a clear code of conduct or set of norms and protocols for behaviour.
- ▶ Recognize and reward performance.
- ▶ Use visuals in communications during desktop video conferencing. Remember the old adage that a picture tells a thousand words.

Adapted from Gould, D (2006) *Virtual Teams* at
www.seanet.com/~daveg/vrteams.htm

How do teams develop?

Coming together is a beginning; keeping together is progress; working together is success.

Henry Ford

From the Project Director:

The most powerful tool for developing the team is communication. You need to strike the balance between keeping team members well informed but not overloading them with too much information. Even over seven weeks of a project, the team develops. People make friends and socialize outside of the project. Friendships dissolve. People are transformed. They find new horizons.

Cog's Ladder, developed by Charrier, and Tuckman's model of team formation both address the question of how teams develop over time.

WHY TWO MODELS?

The two models are described so you can understand better how teams develop. While both describe a similar process, there are sufficient differences in emphasis to make the inclusion of both worthwhile.

Here's a comparison of the stages in both models.

Tuckman (1965) 'Forming-storming-norming-performing'	Charrier (1972) Cog's Ladder
Forming	1 Polite stage; 2 Why we're here stage
Storming	Power stage
Norming	Co-operation stage
Performing	Esprit stage

Added later in 1977 to Tuckman's model was Mourning or Adjourning.

Here you can see clearly the similar structure between the two models. While Cog's Ladder has five stages, the first two stages correspond to Tuckman's 'Forming' stage, for comparison purposes.

The highest stage of the Performing or the Esprit phase will not always be achieved. To reach this level where the team performs smoothly and effectively with high interdependence, the first four phases must have been completed.

In 1977, Tuckman, added a fifth stage: **adjourning** that involves completing the task and breaking up the team. Others call it the phase for mourning.

Insight

As an aside, it is interesting to note that if you want your model to stand out from the crowd, then it helps to make it catchy or rhyming, as in Tuckman's. See later also de Bono's Thinking Hats and Dellinger's *Psycho-Geometrics*®with their respective use of colour and shape.

COG'S LADDER

Cog's Ladder, a model of team development, is based on the work, *Cog's Ladder: A Model of Group Growth*, by George O. Charrier, who published it in the Procter and Gamble company newsletter in 1972, where he was an employee. It is now widely used by businesses to help understand team development.

Cog's Ladder stages

Cog's Ladder describes five steps necessary for a team to be able to work efficiently together. These stages are:

▶ the polite stage
▶ the why we're here stage

- ▶ the power stage
- ▶ the co-operation stage
- ▶ the esprit stage.

Teams can only move forward after completing the current stage.

POLITE STAGE
During this introductory phase, team members strive to get acquainted or reacquainted with one another. Here, the basis for the team structure is established and is characterized by polite social interaction. All ideas are simple, controversy is avoided and all members limit self-disclosure. Judgements of other members are formed and this sets the tone for the rest of the team's time.

WHY WE'RE HERE STAGE
Team members will want to know why they have been called together. The specific agenda for each planning session will be communicated by the team leader. In this phase, individual need for approval begins to diminish as the members examine their team's purpose and begin to set goals. Often, social cliques will begin to form as members begin to feel as though they 'fit in'.

POWER STAGE
Bids for power begin between team members in an effort to convince each other that their position on an issue is correct. Often the field of candidates vying for leadership narrows, as fewer members strive to establish power. Some of those who contributed freely to the team discussion in earlier stages now remain silent, wishing not to engage in a power struggle. It is noted that interactions arising out of this phase do not usually result in optimum solutions. Hence, there is a great need for structure and patience in this stage.

CO-OPERATION STAGE
Team members not only begin to accept that others have an opinion worth expressing, but a team spirit replaces vested interests. Often, new levels of creativity are achieved and the team's productivity soars. If new individuals are introduced into the membership at this point, they will be viewed as outsiders or intruders and the team will have to evolve again, much as it did initially.

ESPRIT STAGE
The esprit stage is about *esprit de corps* which roughly translates as 'team spirit'. (Henri Fayol's golden rule is closely associated with

this stage of Cog's Ladder. It says that nothing has higher pinnacles to reach than *esprit de corps*.) This stage is characterized by mutual acceptance with high cohesiveness and a general feeling of *esprit de corps*. Charrier states that the team can do its finest work and be most productive in this final stage. This stage will not always be achieved. However, to reach this level of co-operation and productivity, the other four stages must have first been met.

Adapted from Charrier, G.O. (1972), *Cog's Ladder: A Model of Group Growth,* Proctor and Gamble company newsletter

TUCKMAN'S GROUP DEVELOPMENT MODEL

The Forming – Storming – Norming – Performing model of group development was first proposed by Bruce Tuckman in 1965 (*Developmental Sequence in Small Groups*, (Psychological Bulletin 63, pp384–399, 1965). Tuckman maintained that these phases are all necessary and inevitable in order for the team:

- ▶ to grow
- ▶ to face up to challenges
- ▶ to tackle problems
- ▶ to find solutions
- ▶ to plan work
- ▶ to deliver results.

... as the team develops maturity and ability, relationships establish and the leader changes leadership style. Beginning with a directing style, moving through coaching, then participating, finishing delegating and almost detached. At this point the team may produce a successor leader and the previous leader can move on to develop a new team.

www.businessballs.com

Forming

In the first stages of team building, the forming of the team takes place. The individual's behaviour is driven by a desire to be accepted by the others and avoid controversy or conflict. Serious issues and feelings are avoided and people focus on being busy with routines, such as team organization, who does what, when to meet, etc.

But individuals are also gathering information and impressions – about each other and about the scope of the task and how to approach it. This is a comfortable stage to be in, but the avoidance of conflict and threat means that not much actually gets done.

The team meets and learns about the opportunities and challenges and then agrees on goals and begins to tackle the tasks. Team members tend to behave quite independently. They may be motivated but are usually relatively uninformed of the issues and objectives of the team. Team members are usually on their best behaviour but very focused on themselves. Mature team members begin to model appropriate behaviour even at this early phase. Sharing the knowledge of the concept of 'Forming, Storming, Norming, Performing' is extremely helpful to the team.

Insight

Team leaders usually need to be directive during this phase.

The forming stage of any team is important because, in this stage, the members of the team get to know one another, exchange some personal information and make new friends. This is also a good opportunity to see how each member of the team works as an individual and how they respond to pressure.

Storming

Every team will next enter the storming stage in which different ideas compete for consideration. The team addresses issues such as what problems they are really supposed to solve, how they will function independently and together and what leadership model they will accept. Team members open up to each other and confront each other's ideas and perspectives.

In some cases storming can be resolved quickly. In others, the team never leaves this stage. The maturity of some team members usually determines whether the team will ever move out of this stage. Some team members will focus on minutiae to evade real issues.

The storming stage is necessary to the growth of the team. It can be contentious, unpleasant and even painful to team members who prefer to avoid conflict. Tolerance of each team member and their differences should be emphasized. Without tolerance and patience the team will fail.

This phase can become destructive to the team and will lower motivation if allowed to get out of control.

The team members will therefore resolve their differences and members will be able to participate with one another more comfortably. The ideal is that they will not feel that they are being judged and will therefore share their opinions and views.

Norming

The team manages to have one goal and come to a mutual plan for the team at this stage. Some may have to give up their own ideas and agree with others in order to make the team function. In this stage, all team members take the responsibility and have the ambition to work for the success of the team's goals.

Performing

It is possible for some teams to reach the performing stage. These high-performing teams are able to function as a unit as they find ways to get the job done smoothly and effectively without inappropriate conflict or the need for external supervision. Team members have become interdependent. By this time, they are motivated and knowledgeable. The team members are now competent, autonomous and able to handle the decision-making process without supervision. Dissent is expected and allowed, as long as it is channelled through means acceptable to the team.

The team will make most of the necessary decisions. Even the most high-performing teams will revert to earlier stages in certain circumstances.

Many long-standing teams go through these cycles many times as they react to changing circumstances. For example, a change in leadership may cause the team to revert to 'storming' as the new people challenge the existing norms and dynamics of the team.

Adjourning and transforming

In 1977, Tuckman, jointly with Mary Ann Jensen, added a fifth stage to the four stages – adjourning – that involves completing the task and breaking up the team. Others call it the phase for mourning.

A team that lasts may transcend to a transforming phase of achievement. Transformational management can produce major changes in performance through synergy and is considered to be more far-reaching than transactional management, where the team members are part of a well defined chain of command and essentially do what the team leader tells them to.

> ### Exercise
> ▶ Using Cog's Ladder or Tuckmann, what stage do you think your team is at?
> ▶ What does this stage feel like? If there's conflict how will you resolve it?

Here are some practical questions that often come up in teamworking.

▶ How do you add new people to a project?

What often happens during a project is that new people join the team. When this happens, what is the best way to introduce someone new into the existing team? Should the process be the same as the first time the team formed or is it different? If so, in what ways? Is it a faster process or a longer one?

▶ How do you reorganize and retain successful teams?

Another frequent event is project reorganization. How do you reorganize and retain successful teams? Do you have to go through the entire team formation process or is there a different team reformation process? Is this faster than the initial process?

> ### Exercise
> ▶ How do you rebuild teams where they have already failed?
> ▶ How do you transform into successful teams those teams that did not have time to successfully form?
>
> See how Cog's Ladder and Tuckman's Five Stages can help you try and answer these challenging questions.

It's not possible to give a simple answer, as that will always depend on individual circumstances. But usually the answer is that where you have a new team member or need to reorganize the team, you will need to allow the team to go through the formation stage again. It may not take quite so long but there are no shortcuts. Teams that are not allowed the time to develop along the lines of Cog's Ladder or Tuckman's Five Stages are unlikely to succeed or last.

Insight

In 1998, Bruce Tuckman's model was adopted by the Boy Scouts of America syllabus for the Wood Badge in place of 'Situational Leadership' which required the payment of royalties for each Scout attending Wood Badge nationwide. See Chapter 3 'How to become a successful team leader'.

As you can see, Cog's Ladder is very similar to Tuckman's model. These are the two most popular models but there are also other similar models such as Tubb, Fisher or Jones, some of which are cyclic rather than reaching an end state.

How to think together as a team

SIX THINKING HATS

Six Thinking Hats is a powerful technique you can use for decision-making from a number of important perspectives. This forces you to move outside your habitual thinking style and helps you to get a more rounded view of a situation. This tool was created by Edward de Bono in his book *Six Thinking Hats* (Viking, 1986).

According to de Bono, many successful people think from a very rational, positive viewpoint. This is part of the reason that they are successful. Often, though, they may fail to look at a problem from an emotional, intuitive, creative or negative viewpoint. This can mean that they underestimate resistance to plans or fail to make creative leaps. Similarly, pessimists may be excessively defensive and more emotional people may fail to look at decisions calmly and rationally.

If you look at a problem with the Six Thinking Hats technique, then you will solve it using all approaches. Your decisions and plans will mix ambition, skill in execution, public sensitivity, creativity and good contingency planning.

Combined with the idea of parallel thinking which is associated with it, it provides a means for teams to think together more effectively and a means to plan thinking processes in a detailed and cohesive way.

How to use the tool

You can use Six Thinking Hats in meetings or on your own. In meetings it has the benefit of blocking the confrontations that happen when people with different thinking styles discuss the same problem. Six distinct states are identified and assigned a colour: each 'Thinking Hat' is a different style of thinking as follows:

WHITE HAT: RATIONAL

Information: considering purely what information is available, what are the facts?

- ▶ With this thinking hat, you focus on the data available.
- ▶ Look at the information you have, and see what you can learn from it.
- ▶ Look for gaps in your knowledge, and either try to fill them or take account of them.
- ▶ This is where you analyse past trends in order to predict future ones.

Examples of White Hat thinking:

- ▶ Total sales of this product are £x per annum.
- ▶ Our sales data is two years old.
- ▶ Energy efficiency legislation is expected to impact our ability to run our business in the next five years.
- ▶ The number of elderly people in Europe is increasing.

RED HAT: EMOTIONAL

Emotions: instinctive gut reaction or statements of emotional feeling (but not any justification).

- ▶ Wearing the red hat, you look at problems using intuition, gut reaction and emotion.
- ▶ Try to think how other people will react emotionally.
- ▶ Try to understand the responses of people who do not fully know your reasoning.

Examples of Red Hat thinking:

- ▶ I'm enthusiastic about getting involved in selling!
- ▶ That role in the company doesn't appeal to me.
- ▶ I'd like to do that but I feel uncertain about it.
- ▶ I'm frustrated that you have let the situation get this bad!

BLACK HAT: PESSIMISTIC

Bad points judgement: logic applied to identifying flaws or barriers, seeking mismatch.

- Using black hat thinking, look at all the bad points of the decision.
- Look at it cautiously and defensively.
- Try to see why it might not work.
- This is important because it highlights the weak points in a plan.
- It allows you to eliminate them, alter them, or prepare plans to counter them.

Black Hat thinking is one of the real benefits of this technique, as many successful people get so used to thinking positively that often they cannot see problems in advance. This leaves them under-prepared for difficulties.

Examples of Black Hat thinking:

- We will be facing strong competition in that market.
- What if you cannot get enough capital together to support the investment?
- We might not be able to make it cheaply enough for our customers to buy it.
- There will be too much political opposition to this approach.
- There is a risk that new legislation will make this market unattractive.

YELLOW HAT: OPTIMISTIC

Good points judgment: logic applied to identifying benefits, seeking harmony.

- The yellow hat helps you to think positively.
- It is the optimistic viewpoint helping you see all the benefits and value of the decision.
- Yellow Hat thinking helps you to keep going when everything looks gloomy and difficult.

Examples of Yellow Hat thinking:

- That would be useful in market X.
- That would reduce the environmental impact of our activities.
- This approach will make our operations more efficient.
- We could use our existing distribution channels for this product.

GREEN HAT: CREATIVE

Creativity: statements of provocation and investigation, seeing where a thought goes.

- ▶ This is where you can develop creative solutions to a problem.
- ▶ It is a freewheeling way of thinking in which there is little criticism of ideas.
- ▶ A whole range of creativity tools can help you here.

Examples of Green Hat thinking:

- ▶ What if you provided it for free?
- ▶ Could you achieve it using technology X instead?
- ▶ If you extended the course by half a day it would really help people understand.
- ▶ How would someone from profession X view this?

BLUE HAT: ORGANIZATIONAL

Thinking: thinking about thinking.

- ▶ The Blue Hat stands for process control.
- ▶ This is the hat worn by people chairing meetings.
- ▶ When running into difficulties because ideas are running dry, they may direct activity into Green Hat thinking.
- ▶ When contingency plans are needed, they will ask for Black Hat thinking, etc.

Examples of Blue Hat thinking:

- ▶ We'll follow this programme of thinking to start the day – does everyone agree?
- ▶ OK. Time to move on to some Yellow Hat thinking.
- ▶ Stop there – you are getting into debate. Let's do some Black Hat thinking and surface all the issues together first.
- ▶ I think you need to revisit our objectives, I'm not sure that they are right in light of our work so far.

All of these thinking hats help encourage thinking more deeply. The Six Thinking Hats indicates problems and solutions about an idea or a product you might come up with. The coloured hats are used as metaphors for each state. Switching to a state is symbolized by the act of putting on a coloured hat, either literally or metaphorically. These metaphors allow for more complete and elaborate segregation of the different thinking states than the preconceptions which exist in people's current language.

It is important to realize that team members all wear the same coloured hat at the same time at the same stage in the process, changing hats as the process moves from stage to stage. They do not wear different coloured hats at the same stage in the process.

Parallel thinking

The Six Thinking Hats process attempts to introduce parallel thinking and structure.

Even with courtesy and clear, shared objectives, in any collaborative thinking activity there is a natural tendency for 'spaghetti thinking' – where one person is thinking about the benefits while another considers the facts and so on. The hats allow this to be avoided so that everyone considers the problems or the benefits or the facts together, reducing distractions and supporting the cross-pollination of thought.

This is achieved because everyone puts on the same hat together e.g. the white hat (rational), then they will all put on the next hat together. In this way everyone thinks in the same way at the same time. The only exception being the facilitator who will tend to keep the blue hat (organizational) on all the time to make sure things progress effectively. The blue hat tends to be the outward looking, leader/trail blazing hat that attracts the leaders of all teams.

Strategies and programmes

Distinct programmes can be created. These are sequences of hats which structure the thinking process towards a distinct goal. Sequences always begin and end with a blue hat. The team agrees the process together:

- ▶ how they will think
- ▶ then they do the thinking
- ▶ then they evaluate the outcomes of that thinking
- ▶ then they agree what they should do next.

Sequences (and indeed hats) may be used by individuals working alone or in groups.

De Bono believes that the key to successful use of the Six Thinking Hats methodology was the deliberate focusing of the discussion on a particular approach as needed during the meeting or session. For instance, a meeting may be called to review a particular problem and to develop a solution for the problem.

The Six Thinking Hats method could then be used in a sequence to:

▶ explore the problem
▶ develop a set of solutions
▶ choose a solution through critical examination of the solution set.

So the meeting may start with everyone assuming the **Blue** Hat (organizational) to discuss how the meeting will be conducted and to develop the goals and objectives.

The discussion may then move to **Red** Hat (emotional) thinking in order to collect opinions and reactions to the problem.

This phase may also be used to develop constraints for the actual solution, such as who will be affected by the problem and/or solutions. Next the discussion may move to the **Yellow** (optimistic) then **Green** (creative) Hats in order to generate ideas and possible solutions.

Next the discussion may move between **White** Hat (rational) thinking as part of developing information and **Black** Hat (pessimistic) thinking to develop criticisms of the solution.

Because everyone is focused on a particular approach at any one time, the team tends to be more collaborative than if one person is reacting emotionally (Red Hat) while another person is trying to be objective (White Hat) and still another person is being critical of the points emerging from the discussion (Black Hat).

Key points:

▶ Six Thinking Hats is a good technique for looking at the effects of a decision from a number of different points of view.
▶ It allows necessary emotion and scepticism to be brought into what would otherwise be purely rational decisions.

- It opens up the opportunity for creativity within decision-making. The technique helps, for example, persistently pessimistic people to be positive and creative.
- Plans developed using this technique will be sounder and more resilient than would otherwise be the case.
- It may also help you to avoid public relations mistakes and spot good reasons not to follow a course of action before you have committed to it.

Adapted from De Bono, E. *Six Thinking Hats*, (Viking, 1986)

Insight

While Cog's Ladder and Tuckman help you understand how teams develop, Six Thinking Hats helps existing teams think in a more organized and effective manner.

Exercise
- Do you imagine you could use Six Thinking Hats with your team for problem-solving?
- How do you think it can help you clarify your team's thinking?

KEYS TO A WINNING TEAM

Which type of team are you in? Different types of teams exist:

- new or existing teams

- independent or interdependent teams

- inter- or multi-disciplinary teams

- project teams.

How well do virtual teams work?

- Team members do not share the same physical location.

- Communicate electronically rather than face-to-face, nationally or even globally.

How do self-managed teams work?

- Can a team be leaderless? Can it be leaderless during its formation?

- They are hard at first, but productive once they take off.

Teams develop in stages as illustrated by:

- Cog's Ladder

- Tuckman's 'Forming, Storming, Norming, Performing'.

How to think together as a team:

- De Bono's Six Thinking Hats model provides a way for teams to think together more effectively and to plan thinking processes in a detailed and cohesive way.

How to help your team succeed

In this chapter you will learn:
- *why some teams succeed while others fail*
- *how you can lead your team members successfully*
- *how to motivate your team.*

This goes to the heart of this book's message: that as an excellent team leader you can make a real difference to your team's performance and therefore make a major contribution to your organization as a whole.

How do you set objectives and measure outcomes so you motivate your team members to perform well? And what is the best way to recognize or reward their efforts?

To help your team succeed you will need to:

▶ understand the different personalities in your team
▶ learn how to assign them to the roles to which they're best suited
▶ set clear objectives and check that they are met
▶ focus on the outcomes
▶ be able to motivate your team
▶ know how to recognize and reward their efforts.

The first two points were covered in Chapter 4 'How to create a balanced team'. This chapter will explain how you can learn to achieve success in the other four areas. But first, take a look at what success feels like to the people who took part in our research.

What does success feel like?

Teamwork divides the task and doubles the success.

Unknown

From the Dancer:

Success means working together, making compromises, listening. You have to search for what is right to make it work. Success for a dancer is when everything looks good, clean and tidy. The formation is good. Everyone is in the right spot.

From the Project Director:

Success means:

... getting it done with consensus and belonging, e.g. youth development – don't let them become disengaged

... all team members functioning at their best. They need to feel comfortable and valued. Then they will feel motivated.

Part of the team leader's role is planning and removing obstacles from the path of the team. Examples are: opening channels; communicating with community partners; picking projects; securing funding to make the service better.

From the Air Traffic Controller:

The objectives of the work are determined at the beginning. The team is successful when the objectives have been achieved, even if the objectives have been reassessed and changed at some intervening stage.

What does failure feel like?

From the Air Traffic Controller:

Failure is not reaching the goal or not functioning as a team.

From the Project Director:

The project goes wrong when the team leader does everything by herself and doesn't delegate; or where there are two team leaders and the team members don't know which one to follow.

From the Banker:

> *The team leader did everything by herself to reach target. She didn't delegate enough. She failed to understand other peoples' capabilities.*

> *The management culture was bullying with heavy pressure on the team to report sales figures daily. But there was no focus on the people – just on the activity.*

Set objectives and focus on the outcomes

From the Banker:

> *Team members need individual goals. But these also need to be flexible enough to allow other priorities to intervene when circumstances change.*

> *Here's an example. A team member is currently targeted on sales and generating income. However, she is very experienced in saving businesses in trouble. So when the credit crunch came, it made sense to switch her away from her sales target towards making better and more immediate use of her skills on debt reduction.*

> *The result is a better service to customers in trouble and greater savings to the bank from rescued businesses. There's a need to be flexible and balanced.*

From the Lead Artist:

> *Set the timeframe at the team meeting: 'What you will do today', 'Who does what?' Then go for it. This frees the team leader to participate rather than spend all her time explaining.*

From the Air Traffic Controller:

> *Without goals (or objectives) team members will be unsure when they have completed their task. If they continue to work on an aspect of the plan when it has already been achieved then they are wasting effort that could have been diverted to more productive work.*

Setting objectives to channel the team's behaviour in a productive direction plays an important part in motivating team members.

Giving individual members achievable targets gives them definite objectives to aim for. This leads them to feel more motivated to try that bit harder.

Objectives seek to answer the question 'Where do you want to go?' They:

▶ enable the team to control its plan
▶ motivate individuals and teams to reach a common goal
▶ provide an agreed, consistent focus for everyone in the team.

SMART OBJECTIVES

All objectives should be **SMART**, which stands for:

▶ Specific
▶ Measurable
▶ Achievable
▶ Realistic
▶ Timely

Specific	Are you precise about what the team is going to achieve?
Measurable	Can you quantify the team's objectives?
Achievable	Is the team attempting too much?
Realistic	Does the team have the resources to make the objective happen ((wo)men, money, machines, materials, minutes)?
Timely	Can you state by when the team will achieve the objective (within ten minutes, a month, by February 2013)?

SMART objectives may be set for profitability, market share, promotional purposes, growth, branding or simply for survival, e.g. 'to survive the downturn' or 'to increase the size of our operation from £200,000 in 2012 to £400,000 in 2013.'

Credited to George T. Doran, *There's a S. M. A. R. T. Way to Write Management Goals and Objectives,* (Management Review, AMA Forum, pp 35–36, 1981).

Be careful not to confuse objectives with goals and aims. Goals and aims tend to be vaguer and focus on the longer term. They will not be

SMART. Strategy is linked to planning. Strategy takes the top view, the so called helicopter view. It provides the overall direction at the highest level. Once you have a strategy, planning is the way to achieve it.

> **Exercise**
> ▶ Do you always know where you want to go?
> ▶ Do you set realistic and achievable objectives?
> ▶ Are they measurable?
> ▶ Think about the objectives you set with your team. Could they be SMARTER?

Motivate the team

> *Money may get you to work but it doesn't get you to work once you're there.*
>
> Unknown

From the Banker:

> *Given encouragement, people can do so much more.*

From the RAF Officer:

> *Create an ethos that they are all part of the team and that all of the work is important. Success in the complex jobs is completely wasted if someone fails to complete the simple but necessary jobs. Treat all team members with respect and solicit their opinions on a regular basis. Even if you do not agree with them, it is useful to know what their opinions are so that you can bring them back on board.*

The lesson here is to motivate your team by leading from the front and by example. You need to be motivated to motivate.

> **Insight**
> Two of the biggest motivators turn out not to be money at all. The first is a sense that your value to the organization is recognized. The second is the belief that you can grow within the organization to fulfil your potential.

It is worth going into a little motivational theory in order to understand clearly its strengths and limits.

Motivation is the act of getting people to do willingly and well the things that need to be done. Most people are motivated by example, especially if it comes from above, e.g. a team leader or a supervisor. It's probably fair to say that the most motivated companies have the most motivated team leaders. Perhaps unsurprisingly, good motivators turn out to have the same qualities as team leaders. These include being trusted, understanding their people and sharing success.

Team leaders who begin meetings by saying, 'OK, let's get this over with as fast as possible so you can get back to our real work,' won't motivate their team. You have to set an example to your team and you can do so by remembering the following key points regarding motivation:

▶ You need to apply yourself to your task and set an example to your team, e.g. take time to prepare for the meeting.
▶ You need to think positively. Repeat to yourself 'My team has the ability to carry out this task.'
▶ You need enthusiasm for your role. Enthusiasm is catching!

Motivation requires an objective:

▶ The objective must be clearly defined, with everybody knowing the part they are to play in achieving it.
▶ The challenge must be achievable. An objective that cannot be achieved is demotivating.

Motivation needs recognition:

▶ People will work harder for recognition than they will for money.
▶ The power of recognition should never be underestimated. Encourage your team members to relate their success stories to their colleagues at your meetings and praise them for a job well done.

Teamwork motivates:

▶ It binds people together.
▶ It encourages a competitive spirit.
▶ It gives them a common objective.

You can be motivated in a repetitive job if:

▶ other people recognize the importance of your role in the wider scheme of things
▶ you recognize the importance of your role in the wider scheme of things.

Don't get into the habit of seeing your role as routine and the role of others as glamorous. The person who stuffs envelopes for a mailout is as important as the person who composes the letter!

Motivation never lasts:

▶ You can inflate a balloon and tie it at the top but after a time it will begin to deflate and you'll need to inflate it again. Likewise, motivation needs to be topped up regularly.
▶ Self-motivation can be given an extra boost with a little self-assessment.

LEARN TO MOTIVATE

▶ Learn to lead by example.
▶ Examine expectations; point the way ahead.
▶ Always show you care; treat people as individuals.
▶ Recognize achievement; acknowledge extra effort.
▶ Never stifle personal growth; set a challenge but make it achievable.

Key points to remember about motivation are:

▶ Motivation is not the only determinant of individual performance but it is an important one. It has been difficult to analyse and define.
▶ The motivation of team members can be influenced by team leaders, i.e. motivation can be managed.
▶ Motivational efforts need to be sensitive to variations in team members' needs, abilities and goals.
▶ Effort increases as the difficulty of the task or goal increases, but there comes a point at which the task is perceived as being too difficult and the effort actually decreases.
▶ People are motivated by a desire to be treated equitably at work. Motivational programmes should be perceived as equitable and achievable.
▶ Appropriate rewards can improve performance.
▶ The motivation strategy should connect an individual's valued outcomes with the desired performance:
  ▷ Can I do it? If I do it, what will be the outcome? Will it be worth it?

- People can be motivated by external events:
  - ▷ Performance will continue if it results in something valued by the performer.
  - ▷ Positive reinforcement is a powerful tool and when used appropriately it can make people repeat their behaviour.
  - ▷ Measurement and feedback are essential to improving performance.

From these points, it is clear that team leaders can influence team member behaviour and that measurement and feedback are essential to improving performance. Therefore the setting of targets is critical to the individual's decision to make the effort to reach the goal.

Insight
There is a point at which the task is perceived as being too difficult and the effort actually decreases.

Motivating the team depends on how well the project is set up in the first place. Where team members are involved in its design then they will be motivated. It's all about engagement.

Recognize great performers

UNDERSTANDING THE VALUE OF RECOGNITION AND REWARD

Good performance means recognizing when people are contributing within their capacity and when they are using their talents to the full. Never underestimate the power of recognition and reward on your team. It is the most powerful motivator you can use both for the individual and for the team as a whole. The only difference between recognition and reward is that one has a cost attached and the other doesn't. Recognition can often be just as powerful as reward.

The ways and means of recognizing people
At one end of the spectrum, you can use a simple thank you, a written memo or public praise at a meeting. At the other end, you might use rewards with a cost attached, such as seats for the theatre or a sporting event. In the middle of the spectrum you might use a simple

gift such as a bunch of flowers or a box of chocolates as a reward for extra effort or a job well done.

Rewards do not have to be expensive. Very often, recognition is just as important. A simple 'Thank you!' or handwritten note may sometimes be more meaningful than a bouquet of fresh flowers delivered every day for a month or a chauffeur-driven Rolls Royce for a week.

You know your team better than anyone and you will know what the most appropriate reward for each of them is. Some acts of recognition cost nothing but can have a hugely motivating effect.

Catch people doing something right for a change, instead of something wrong. Encourage your staff by rewarding or recognizing them and celebrating success.

Making awards
When giving any form of recognition or reward you should:

▶ make awards in public not private
▶ seek the right occasion, e.g. a team meeting or even team lunch
▶ explain to everyone exactly why the award is being made so they know what they need to do to gain one
▶ encourage team members not getting an award to aspire to winning next time; don't let them feel like 'losers'
▶ create a little bit of 'theatre' by making the giving of the award a special event.

Communicating news of recognition and rewards:

▶ Spread the word!
▶ Other people should know when someone has been recognized. This is the key factor in maximizing the effect of rewards on others in the department.
▶ Use existing communication channels such as notice boards, bulletins and newsletters.
▶ Send out a memo for circulation throughout the department.

RECOGNIZING GOOD PERFORMANCE
As a team leader you need to recognize good performance but you also need to correct the behaviour of those who underperform or who just perform badly. Typically at one end of the spectrum you will

have a small number of people whose performance is outstanding. At the other end you will have a small number whose performance is poor. Most people will fall between these two extremes. It's a classic bell-shaped curve.

What tends to happen is that the majority in the middle are neglected while the team leader spends most time with the poor performers and then with the outstanding ones. This ignores the fact that it's the team members whose performance is in the middle who form the backbone of the organization.

By ignoring them, you remove the incentive for them to improve. The number of people at the high and low end is too small to make a significant difference to the performance of the team as a whole. If each individual in the group of middle-ground performers were to increase their contribution by just ten per cent, the impact on the entire organization would be enormous.

When is recognition appropriate?

According to Dick Grote in his book *Discipline without punishment* (Amacom, 2006), there are three situations where recognition of good performance is appropriate:

1 When an individual has done something 'above and beyond the call of duty.'
2 When a team member has significantly improved performance, either after a coaching or disciplinary transaction or by his/her own efforts.
3 When a team member hasn't done anything particularly special or outstanding. The individual has simply met all the organization's expectations over a long period of time.

Since those in this last group are doing exactly what is expected, it is easy to overlook the need for recognition. The team leader's challenge is to find examples of good performance to recognize.

Identifying specific behaviours to recognize

Be specific when recognizing good performance. The test for being specific is to see if you can take a photo or an audio recording of it. If you can, it's specific. If you cannot, it isn't. While you can't take a photo of a good attitude, you can make a recording of someone saying 'Let me help you with that.'

If you cannot tell a team member exactly what it is that causes them to feel good about their performance, the chances are that they will be unable to continue that good performance. By being so specific, these actions may seem unimportant in themselves but good performance consists of doing a great many small things well.

Grote's guidelines for effective recognition are as follows:

1 Recognize good performance often.
2 Recognition is most influential when it rapidly follows the behaviour being reinforced.
3 Recognition is most effective when it is directed to specific individuals rather than to teams or groups of team members.
4 Recognition is most effective when it is tailored to the preferences of the individual. For example, some team members like to have their contributions made known to the group directly. Others prefer that their achievements be acknowledged privately.
5 Recognition needs to be proportionate to the performance. The sincerity and good sense of a team leader who praises a minor contribution lavishly is questioned by the recipient and by others.
6 Don't wait until a person has performed perfectly to provide recognition. Acknowledge the minor achievements that produce the ultimate result.

Recognition tools

Your words are the most important tool you have to influence the performance of others. Simply telling team members that you have noticed and appreciate their good performance in one area of their job makes it more likely that the good performance will continue. Words of thanks and appreciation are simple and cost nothing, e.g. 'Good job,' 'Well done,' 'Thanks,' or 'I really appreciate that.'

Grote suggests the following tools for recognizing performance:

▶ Write a quick thank you on a Post-It note and leave it on the team member's desk.
▶ Write your boss a memo about what the team member is accomplishing and send a copy to the team member.
▶ Ask the team member's advice about a business-related matter, such as how to reduce waste, how to improve customer service, how to reorganize the work flow when someone is out, etc.

- ▶ Assign the team member to work on a desirable project.
- ▶ Introduce the team member to a visitor and explain to the visitor how the team member's work contributes to the success of the department.

Insight

Here are some of the reasons why team leaders don't recognize good performance often enough: 'I'm too busy,' or 'I always expect good performance,' or 'Nobody recognizes my good performance,' or 'I feel awkward telling team members they are doing a good job.'

The most authentic reason many team leaders don't use recognition to motivate improved performance is that recognizing good performance forces team leaders to discriminate among their people – to separate those who are performing well from those who are not.

Don't be a 'treat-everybody-alike' team leader by avoiding this challenge to discriminate between good performers and those whose performance is average or below par.

Grote suggests the following assignment:

1 Once a day, find one team member who is doing exactly what they are supposed to be doing – nothing special, nothing above and beyond the call of duty, just doing what they are paid to do.
2 Tell that person that you noticed that they were doing the job right, say thank you and go back to your desk.
3 Do this every day and see what happens.

Adapted from *Recognizing Good Performance* by Dick Grote from
www.melbabenson.com/articles_files/recognizing.pdf

Exercise
- ▶ Do you always remember to recognize your team members' efforts?
- ▶ How would you describe the difference between recognition and reward?
- ▶ How do you recognize your team members' performance?
- ▶ What rewards do you offer for work well done?
- ▶ Think about the ways you recognize and reward your team members.

Dealing with customer praise

Most companies have a process for dealing with customer complaints. But what about *praise* from customers? How about catching a team member doing something right! This is all too often overlooked or goes unrecognized. Andy Hanselman thinks organizations can learn to handle customer praise better and suggests five ideas for you to consider:

Idea 1: Appoint someone with responsibility for handling customer praise.

Their job is to formally review all positive customer comments and make sure that they get acknowledged.

Idea 2: Put customer praise on the agenda.

See that good customer service examples get mentioned everywhere – in team meetings, newsletters and intranets.

Idea 3: Spot your people doing things well.

Recognize them publically or in private and really make people feel valued.

Idea 4: Make it public.

What can you do formally to recognize outstanding individual customer service performances? When was the last time you actually did it?

Examples might be an 'Oscars' ceremony to recognize great individual performances from the past year, as voted by their peers, or a reserved car parking space for the 'employee of the month'. How do you recognize your outstanding employees?

Idea 5: Get your customers to do it for you.

What about a direct reward for excellent customer service? Hanselman quotes two examples:

1 An airline that sent vouchers to their customers to give to members of staff who made their trip an enjoyable one.
2 A hotel he was staying at where he was given a token that he had to give to the person who made his stay a great one. Staff could then exchange the token for a reward.

Could either of these ideas work in your organization?

Ask your customers to nominate your best performers and send them a voucher they can give to your team. This demonstrates you believe in great service, it highlights brilliant performers and it engages your customers.

Adapted from Andy Hanselman Consulting from Businesszone
www.businesszone.co.uk/blogs/andyhanselman/compete-or-get-beat/happy-customers-5-ideas-deal-them

'Inspiring team members' checklist

Answer the questions in this checklist (on the following pages) to find out how inspiring you are as a team leader. Place a tick in the column that matches your response for each question. You may wish to photocopy the quiz and use the copy as your score sheet. You can also ask your team members to complete the checklist as a team exercise and then combine the answers into a team response.

Step 1: Scoring

▶ Add up all the ticks in the 'Always' column then multiply them by 4.
▶ Add up all the ticks in the 'Frequently' column then multiply them by 3.
▶ Add up all the ticks in the 'Occasionally' column then multiply them by 2.
▶ Add up all the ticks in the 'Never' column then multiply them by 1.

Step 2: Add together the totals for all four columns to give a final score.

Step 3: Draw conclusions

0 - 20	Never inspiring
21 - 40	Occasionally inspiring
41 - 60	Frequently inspiring
61 - 80	Well done! Always inspiring

WHAT'S IN IT FOR YOU, THE TEAM LEADER?

Being an effective team leader brings extra responsibilities, and the job requires time to be done well. It does, however, bring its own benefits.

Inspiring team members checklist

	Always	Frequently	Occasionally	Never
1 Are you highly motivated yourself?				
2 Are you enthusiastic?				
3 Do you think positively?				
4 Do you set clear objectives?				
5 Are the objectives you set achievable?				
6 Do you recognize your team's efforts?				
7 Do you maintain momentum?				
8 Do you guide and inspire your team?				
9 Are you loyal to the team?				
10 Are you sensitive to the needs and views of others?				
11 Are you genuinely interested in the development of others?				
12 Are you assertive?				
13 Do you help others to find answers?				
14 Do you give people the opportunity to grow?				
15 Do you ask questions more than giving answers?				

	Always	Frequently	Occasionally	Never
16 Do you delegate the task and the authority?				
17 Do you raise people's self-esteem?				
18 Do you give people the opportunity to get it wrong if necessary?				
19 Do you listen more than you talk?				
20 Do you recognize good performance?				
Total	= ticks × 4	= ticks × 3	= ticks × 2	= ticks × 1

Half the battle lies in getting the groundwork done properly. The other half is leading from the front by providing a motivating and inspiring role model for your team to emulate.

By practising the three key issues of inspiring team members, providing a motivational role model and maximizing the effects of reward and recognition you will:

▶ build a positive, highly motivated team who always give their best
▶ contribute significantly to your quality goals
▶ be an effective and professional leader.

Practise your team leadership skills and everyone wins; the customer, the company, the team and, last but not least, you, the team leader. It's not complicated and much is common sense but it does require constant application to get into good habits.

KEYS TO A WINNING TEAM

What does success feel like?

- 'Success means getting it done with consensus and belonging with all your team members functioning at their best. They need to feel comfortable and valued. Then they will feel motivated.' (Lead Artist)

Why set objectives and focus on the outcomes?

- Objectives seek to answer the question 'Where do you want to go?'

- All objectives should be *SMART*, standing for: Specific; Measurable; Achievable; Realistic; Timely.

- They motivate individuals and teams to reach a common goal.

- They provide an agreed, consistent focus for everyone in the team.

Motivate the team:

- 'Given encouragement, people can do so much more.' (Banker)

- Most people are motivated by example.

- Apply yourself to your task to set an example for your team.

- Show enthusiasm for your role. Enthusiasm is catching!

- Think positively: 'My team has got the ability to carry out this task.'

- Motivation requires an achievable objective.

Recognize great performers:

- Recognize good performance often.

- Recognition is most influential when it rapidly follows the behaviour being reinforced and is directed to specific individuals rather than to teams.

- Acknowledge minor achievements.

- Don't wait for someone to perform perfectly before providing recognition.

How to improve your teamwork skills

In this chapter you will learn:
- *the social skills you need to function fluently with your team*
- *other key skills you need to be a successful team leader*
- *what additional skills you should seek to develop as you grow into the team leader role.*

Research on the type of skills needed by a team leader produced the following results.

From the Air Traffic Controller:

What are the three most important skills you need as a team leader?

1 *To have a clear idea of the objectives and communicate this effectively to the team.*
2 *To maintain an overview and identify changes that need to be made.*
3 *To identify strengths and weaknesses within your team.*

How can you improve your skills as a leader or communicator?

Start off with the premise that you are not always right just because you are the team leader. Constantly question yourself. Where criticism comes from a team member, do not just dismiss it. Listen to what they say and if the criticism is correct, acknowledge it and implement the changes required. If you don't agree, show respect for the point raised and give a logical reason as to why you discounted it.

From the Project Director:

What are the three most important skills you need as a team leader?

Listening, communicating and being well organized.

How can you improve your skills as a leader or communicator?

You can improve by reflective practice and evaluating what you have done at all times. You can use a 360-degree type appraisal with the director's assistant and team members.

You should have clear objectives but then not micromanage, e.g. by going round telling people to work faster and they say: 'This doesn't help. Don't worry we'll finish in time.' Have trust in the team and don't transfer your anxieties onto the team members.

How important is planning? How do you learn to plan?

The team leader should create the master plan with vision. This can possibly be trained – e.g. principles of Project Management like Critical Path Analysis – so the team leader learns foresight but it must always be allied to practice.

What other skills do you think are important?

Stay positive at all times!

From the Dancer:

What teamwork skills do you need?

You need:

- ▶ *the ability to communicate objectives clearly*
- ▶ *commitment, organization and motivation*
- ▶ *experience to know which battles to fight and which to avoid*
- ▶ *time management*
- ▶ *dedication*
- ▶ *belief in the work and love for it too*
- ▶ *firmness and strictness, e.g. don't be afraid to lay down the law.*

Planning is very important. You learn this by organizing your time and knowing how long things take and allowing enough time.

From the Banker:

What teamwork skills do you need most?

The ability to understand team members' differences, skill sets and motivation.

You need to:

▶ *lead from the front*
▶ *live and breathe what the team does, or else they cannot buy in*
▶ *energize the team to drive growth and create opportunities.*

It's important you know how to speak well in public so try to get plenty of practice in making presentations. Improve your skills, get constructive feedback and establish what to work on. Ask for open feedback from your manager and accept it. Look for opportunities to develop your leadership skills. Other skills are energy and stamina so try to keep fit by, for example, swimming at lunch time.

You should set individual measurable objectives but also be focused on team performance. Be flexible where circumstances change.

Diversity: you must respect gender/race/country/disability – the individually talented. For example, the credit team may transcend different countries. They have a virtual team with 100 people in Calcutta.

What skills do you need?

Team leaders need a variety of basic social skills to make the team work effectively. These are the social lubricants that oil the interactions between you and your team members and which keep everything running smoothly.

Before detailing specific core skills for listening, communicating, building trust and planning, let's consider the more invisible skill of emotional intelligence. Chapter 2 talked about emotional strength being at the heart of the team and underpinning all other values. In fact, it's worth quoting John Frost again:

Without exception, the teams that sustain performance over time are the ones that invest in the emotional foundations first. They understand that when the emotional connection is made, when the team decides what it wants to be, then achieving what it wants to do follows naturally.

John Frost, *HR Initiatives Newsletter 2009*

Now we're talking about emotional intelligence. This remains a highly controversial subject with many different theories. Basically it refers to your ability to perceive, use, understand and manage your emotions.

Goleman's model, as shown in the table below and in Figure 7.1, provides a good basis for understanding emotional intelligence.

	What I see	*What I do*
Personal competence	Self-awareness	Self-management
Social competence	Social awareness	Relationship management

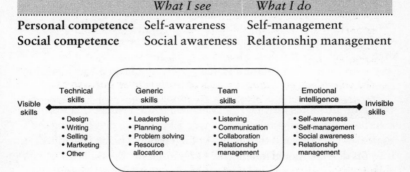

Figure. 7.1 A spectrum of skills needed for teamwork.

Insight

Go to www.myskillsprofile.com for an online test to define your emotional intelligence with a 136-question test that should take you about 20 minutes to complete.

DOES EMOTIONAL INTELLIGENCE AFFECT SUCCESSFUL TEAMWORK?

In their paper, *Does emotional intelligence affect successful teamwork?* (Edith Cowan University, Australia, 2001), Joe Luca and Pina Tarricone describe an experiment where college students were required to complete a genuine project for 'real' clients where teamwork was an essential ingredient. At the end of the project, both successful and unsuccessful teams – judged in terms of collaboration and teamwork – were interviewed to find those factors that led to success. It was found that there was a strong correspondence between students' emotional intelligence and team harmony.

Skills such as problem-solving, communication, collaboration, interpersonal skills, social skills and time management are actively being targeted by prospective employers as essential requirements for employability, especially in team environments. Of these, employers consistently mention collaboration and teamwork as being a critical skill, essential in almost all working environments.

This study analysed the team dynamics of a team that was working well together and one that was not. The successful team was highly motivated to produce a quality product and they were not bothered by personal issues. This team felt that it was a good thing to discuss problems as and when they came up so that they could get on with the job and make sure the final product was not harmed. This team worked positively with each other in an interdependent way with a high degree of interaction. However, the other team did not work well with each other, communicated poorly and lacked consideration, empathy and understanding.

Using the attributes provided by Goleman, it was evident that team members' emotional intelligence played a key role in determining the success of the team and the quality of final product being developed. It seems that emotional intelligence skills underpin the skills for collaborating and communicating that are needed for managing conflict and keeping the team focused on developing the product.

This study shows convincingly the relationship between team members' emotional intelligence and their ability to work effectively within a team. When people are going to work in teams, visible skills and emotional intelligence should both be considered when selecting team members who will work collaboratively. Everyone should be made aware of emotional intelligence and the impact it can have on the team's success.

Luca and Tarricone's framework (on the following pages) was developed from the literature based on students' emotional intelligence and propensity to engage in collaborative teamwork. The table shows definitions for different emotional intelligence factors and relates them to successful teamworking. So, for example, self regulation is defined (in part) as the ability to control disruptive impulses, which relates (in part) to handling emotions and putting the team first.

Emotional Intelligence (modified from Goleman 1998a) and attributes of successful teams

	Definition	Relationship to successful teamwork
Self-awareness	The ability to recognize and understand your moods, emotions and drives, as well as their effect on others	▲ Having positive and productive teamwork skills ▲ Controlling emotions and understand the impact of emotions on the team ▲ Being self-confident, high self-esteem and a coherent and integrated self-identity ▲ Promoting psychological health including a happy disposition
Self-regulation	The ability to control or redirect disruptive impulses and moods; the propensity to suspend judgement – to think before acting	▲ Being self-aware of emotions to enable self-regulation ▲ Handling emotions and putting the team task first ▲ Using emotions to facilitate the progress of the project ▲ Regulating emotions during conflict, pressure, stress and deadlines ▲ Coping with stress, frustrations through creating and contributing to caring, supportive relationships
Motivation	A passion to work for reasons that go beyond money or status; a propensity to pursue goals with energy and persistence	▲ Motivating other team members to contributing their best ▲ Openness, flexibility and motivation to change, innovation, creativity and collaborative problem-solving ▲ Creating an environment that stimulates, enhances and empowers team members to become motivated and apply themselves fully ▲ Showing initiative, perseverance and dedication, goal orientation and focus ▲ Placing team or common goals ahead of individual goals and pursuing these with determination and perseverance ▲ Having a sincere interest and motivation for the group and individual's achievements and goals

	Definition	Relationship to successful teamwork
Empathy	The ability to understand the emotional makeup of other people; skill in treating people according to their emotional reactions	▲ Considering team morale and aiming to maintain a positive, productive work environment ▲ Understanding, interpreting and identifying with colleagues' feelings ▲ Cultivating rapport with people from different 'walks of life' ▲ Having the potential to turn adversarial relationships into collaborative alliances ▲ Showing emotional concern, including reassurance and caring for other team members ▲ Helping to create a team environment where members can express their feelings
Social skill	Proficiency in managing relationships and building networks; an ability to find common ground and build rapport	▲ Creating a team culture which is supportive, informal, comfortable and non-judgemental ▲ Developing professional as well as positive, personal relationships with other team members ▲ Developing intense, short-term relationships and being able to disconnect and work in another team environment with the same sincerity and motivation ▲ Being able to stimulate co-operation, collaboration and teamwork through well-developed communication and social skills ▲ Developing positive, effective relationships with colleagues through fostering trust, confidence and commitment ▲ Helping to establish a positive team climate and promoting support and respect for one another ▲ Having the ability to interact with team members and deter conflict, be aware of, ease and dissipate underlying tensions

Acknowledgements to Joe Luca and Pina Tarricone

Moving on to the team and generic skills, there are a number of basic social skills that a good team leader needs.

Skills	It is important:
Listening	to listen to other people's ideas. When people are allowed to express their ideas freely, these initial ideas will produce other ideas.
Questioning	to ask questions, interact, and discuss the team's objectives.
Persuading	to encourage people to exchange, defend and then ultimately rethink their ideas.
Respecting	to treat others with respect and to support their ideas.
Helping	to help one's co-workers, which is the general theme of teamwork.
Sharing	to share with the team to create a teamworking environment.
Participating	to encourage all members of the team to participate in the team.
Communicating	to work effectively as a team to acquire communication skills to communicate effectively with one another, e.g. using e-mail, team meetings, one-on-one communication and so on. This will enable team members to work together and achieve the team's purpose and objectives.

To these, add the three qualities of trust, assertiveness and adaptability. Trust is about earning significant support and respect from your team. Assertiveness is needed for you to get your ideas across to your team and adaptability is essential so that as the task or situation changes, you can adapt your plan.

As a team leader, you will bring to the team your own skills and abilities. These will probably include many of those in the table above. But there is always room to develop your skills and take them to a higher level. Remember too that all these skills are interrelated and do not stand alone.

More formally defined are the skills listed below, focusing in depth on the first three core skills and more briefly on the last three.

- ▶ Listening: learning and practising the skill of active listening.
- ▶ Communication: receiving and transmitting clear messages.
- ▶ Building trust: depending on each other to achieve a common purpose.
- ▶ Planning: agreeing a plan as a team and following it through.
- ▶ Abstract reasoning: analysing a problem and coming up with a solution.
- ▶ Resource allocation: deciding which resources to use when.
- ▶ Change management: considering that the plan may have to change.

Listening, communication, building trust and planning are core team-leader skills that apply to any task or situation. Without these skills you cannot perform effectively as a team leader and your team will find it almost impossible to work together in harmony.

Listen and communicate better

When people talk, listen completely. Most people never listen.

Ernest Hemingway

ACTIVE LISTENING

Listening is one of the most important skills you can have. How well you listen affects how well you do your job and how good your relationships are with others. Too often, people hear without actively listening. Expect to remember only part of what you hear. When you talk to your team members, they're only listening to part of the conversation too!

The way to become a better listener is to practise 'active listening'. You can do this by making a conscious effort to hear the words the other person is saying but also, more importantly, you are trying to understand the complete message being sent.

When you listen superficially you are liable to get confused, lose track of the conversation or end up having to ask the speaker to repeat what they just said. In conversation, when talking back and forth, you may often be concentrating on making your next point, rather than focusing on what the other person is saying. Avoid the habit of finishing other people's sentences for them and, of course, don't interrupt! All of these contribute to a lack of listening and understanding.

Active listening, on the other hand, means clearing your mind of all other distractions and really tuning in to what the other person is saying, paying attention to the other person very carefully. It takes a lot of concentration and determination to be an active listener.

Becoming an active listener

There are five key elements of active listening. They all help you ensure that you hear the other person, and that the other person knows you are hearing what they say. When listening actively:

- ▶ pay attention
- ▶ show that you are listening
- ▶ provide feedback
- ▶ defer judgement
- ▶ respond appropriately.

COMMUNICATE BETTER

Communication is one of the core teamwork skills and is central to all teamworking. The success or failure of the team will depend, in large part, on how effectively they communicate with each other and with you! This means receiving messages as much as sending messages or, put another way, listening as much as talking.

Sending and receiving clear messages

To understand how to send and receive clear messages more of the time, you need to look at much more than the words you speak. You need to consider:

- ▶ the need for positive attitudes
- ▶ the non-verbal signals that the voice, the face and the body send
- ▶ techniques that establish rapport between us and other people.

Good communication is like words, music and dance all working together. The music is the tone of voice, the dance is the body language and the words are the spoken content. That is, you need to look at all the key components to communicate successfully.

What are the characteristics of good communication?
To work effectively, everyone in the team needs to be a good communicator. In a world of perfect communication you would all live in harmony with one another. You would never hear phrases such as:

- ▶ 'You just don't understand, do you?'
- ▶ 'It's no use talking to him when he's in that mood.'
- ▶ 'That's not what you said at the time.'
- ▶ 'I was afraid to ask.'
- ▶ 'If only she'd bothered to explain it properly.'
- ▶ 'I didn't ask for this.'
- ▶ 'I thought you said… '

All these phrases, in their different ways, indicate a failure to communicate properly and sometimes show a complete breakdown in communication. In the real world, with its pressure and time constraints, everyone, at times, sends and receives messages which are unclear, confused, misleading and just plain wrong. This shows up very clearly in teamworking activities.

Effective communicators on the other hand:

- ▶ show empathy
- ▶ use a tone of voice which shows attention, concern and courtesy
- ▶ have awareness of non-verbal body signals, such as:
    - ▷ shape of the mouth and the angle of the eyebrows
    - ▷ the eyes and the size of the pupils
    - ▷ position of shoulders and head
- ▶ send clear messages by:
    - ▷ taking time to think before speaking
    - ▷ speaking clearly in a language the customer can understand
    - ▷ repeating important messages
- ▶ receive clear messages by:
    - ▷ clearing the mind of 'baggage'
    - ▷ listening actively
    - ▷ not interrupting.

Communication is a two way process. It is not just what you say or write but how you listen as well. Listening is not a passive state. It should be an active, mental process. Active listening plays a crucial role in effective communication.

Words, tone of voice and body language

There are basically three elements in any face-to-face communication:

- ▶ words
- ▶ tone of voice
- ▶ body language.

Insight

It has been often reported that body language and tone of voice are much more important than what is said. It's often quoted that words account for seven per cent of verbal communication, tone of voice 38 per cent and body language 55 per cent. However, as Albert Mehrabian 1971 (currently Professor Emeritus of Psychology, UCLA) has demonstrated, it turns out this applies only to communicating *feelings and attitudes* and not to communications in general.

It does mean, however, that you should make sure your words, tone of voice and body language are all aligned. Where they do not match – for example, you're laughing while saying something sad – your listener will become confused.

It helps if you are aware of who you are talking to so you can vary your verbal behaviour to take account of the team member's own communication style. Asking the right questions is important too.

Build trust and learn to plan

BUILD TRUST

To be trusted is a greater compliment than to be loved.

George MacDonald

If you don't trust people, people will not trust you.

Lao Tzu

It can be said that trust is:

- ▶ a shared belief that you can depend on each other to achieve a common purpose
- ▶ the building block for all relationships
- ▶ where people know they can rely on your word
- ▶ built through integrity and consistency.

People sense how you feel about them. If you want to change their attitudes toward you, change the negative attitudes you have toward them.

If you listen well, people will trust you.

You cannot establish trust if you cannot listen. A conversation is a relationship in which both speaker and listener play a part, each influencing the other. Instead of being a passive recipient, the listener has as much to do in shaping the conversation as the speaker.

Kerry L. Johnson, *Selling with NLP* (Nicholas Brealey Publishing, 1994)

Empathy is relevant to trust because it gives you insights into what others may be feeling or thinking and helps you understand why others are reacting to situations in a particular way. It informs your decisions.

Trust-based working relationships
Trust has an important link with your organizational success.

Trust elevates levels of commitment and sustains effort and performance without the need for management controls and close monitoring.

Kerry L. Johnson, *Selling with NLP* (Nicholas Brealey Publishing, 1994)

Trust between a team leader and a team member is based on the trustor's perception of the trustee's ability, benevolence and integrity. Credibility comes from the head, but trust is a gut reaction.

Building trust means:

▶ sharing important information, especially about oneself
▶ the willingness to be influenced
▶ not taking advantage of team members' weaknesses
▶ being fair
▶ fulfilling promises.

LEARN TO PLAN
It pays to plan ahead. It wasn't raining when Noah built the ark.

Anon

From the Air Traffic Controller:

How important is planning? How do you learn to plan?

It depends on the job in hand but most complex jobs require planning to complete the task in the most efficient manner. You don't want some people with nothing to do while others have too much. Computer-based project planning tools can assist with this. Also, if you want to arrange the correct people to be available at the appropriate times you must have some idea of when sections of the project start and end. Without planning you can't do this.

Teams often plunge in and act before they have taken the time to plan. Under the time pressure to complete a task, it often seems as though getting stuck in is the right thing to do and that spending valuable time planning is a waste of time. You may have heard the carpenter's saying 'measure twice, cut once'. It shows that acting without planning can be expensive. The potential cost of poorly thought out actions can be high, so you should not only plan, but check your plan before you act.

Insight
Don't be like the man who built a boat in his basement only to discover too late that the boat was too big to take out through the basement door.

If you prepare a proper plan, you will have set down markers for yourself and your team. You and the team will know where you are going and how you are going to get there. You and your team will have credibility from the start.

Time spent planning pays off
Designing a business plan is like building a house. You need firm foundations and you can't add the roof without the walls! Successful teams discover that the time they spend in these planning stages is time well spent, as it provides a map you all can follow which will warn you if you stray off course.

Where am I now? Where do I want to be?
Planning is about how you and the team can get from where you are now to where you want to be. Whether this is in the next ten minutes, ten months or even ten years, this is always a good question to ask. For the team, planning needs to answer the 'How?' question: 'How

do you get there?' which involves 'When does this or that have to happen?' and 'Who does what?' An added benefit is that where team members share decisions and have a sense of their own involvement and empowerment, they are more motivated in carrying them out.

An approach to success

Planning in business generally focuses on a particular product, service or project. Drawing up, maintaining and revising the plan is essential for any business (including successful and growing businesses).

Essentially, a business plan is a blueprint for success because it sets out in detail what you believe will happen over the next time period. It lets you check actual events against forecast events so you can adjust the plan as required with the current reality.

This way, the organization will not be caught unawares in an ever-changing economy and won't end up using a tactic that might have worked yesterday but will not work today.

Where do you want to go?

Planning is also about objectives. Objectives seek to answer the question 'Where do you want to go?' They:

▶ enable the business or team to *control* its plan
▶ motivate individuals and teams to reach a common goal
▶ provide an agreed, consistent focus for everyone in the business or team.

For more on objectives, see Chapter 6 'Set objectives and focus on the outcomes'.

Insight
Overcomplicating tasks is a common problem. Simplicity is often the best way forward and careful planning will get you to the simplest solution.

Take time to plan

Exercise
▶ Does your team leap into action too quickly?
▶ Do you and your team spend enough time planning?

Time spent planning will result in better execution. Team members can come to see the need for planning in a very practical and concrete way.

Planning is vital through all aspects of an organization and having a plan is key to your success.

Adding extra skills

From the Air Traffic Controller:

What other skills do you think are important?

Intelligence coupled with common sense. When things go wrong it is important to have a sense of humour and motivate the team to get the job back on the rails.

The last section looks at some of the additional skills you should consider developing as a team leader. These might include:

- ▶ Adaptability: being able to adjust to changing circumstances.
- ▶ Abstract reasoning: analysing a problem to come up with a solution.
- ▶ Analytical/logical thinking: using sound arguments to reach a conclusion.
- ▶ Resource allocation: considering which resources to use when.
- ▶ Responding to change: anticipating that the plan may have to change.
- ▶ Creativity: seeing the task in new ways to create new solutions.
- ▶ Big picture: taking the overview to see things as a whole.

A brief description of each follows.

ADAPTABILITY

The art of life is a constant readjustment to our surroundings.

Kakuzo Okakaura

If you live in the river you should make friends with the crocodile.

Indian proverb

Adaptability means being able to make compromises and to adjust to changing circumstances. Adaptability is the personal characteristic that allows someone to change their behaviour in order to relate better to other people. Adaptability is similar to change, but not to the same degree and in smaller increments. So, for example, adapting a plan is less drastic than changing it. It's all a matter of degrees.

People who are adaptable:

▶ display flexibility and openness and encourage others to stay open to change
▶ adapt their own attitudes and behaviour to work effectively with different people and situations
▶ accept and adapt to changing priorities, better ideas and methods
▶ maintain work effectiveness in new situations.

ABSTRACT REASONING

A little knowledge is a dangerous thing. So is a lot.

Albert Einstein

At its simplest, abstract reasoning is the process of using your mind to consider something carefully. In more formal terms, abstraction is the process of generalization by reducing the information content of a concept or an observable phenomenon. Typically, you do this in order to retain only information which is relevant for a particular purpose.

Abstract reasoning is the ability to separate the whole into its constituent parts in order to study the parts and their relations. This means being able to apply abstract concepts to new situations and surroundings. It's about conceptualizing ideas and then applying them in problem-solving.

Common types of reasoning are:

Deductive reasoning – which is reasoning from the general to the particular. This involves arguing from a general premise to a particular conclusion. So 'All men are mortal; Socrates is a man; Socrates is mortal.' This is only true if the premise is true. But once this is so, the conclusion follows logically and inevitably from the premise.

Inductive reasoning – or inference, which is the reasoning involved in drawing a conclusion or making a logical judgement on the basis of circumstantial evidence and prior conclusions rather than on the basis of direct observation. Here the conclusion is inferred from the probability of the premise. So: 'The sun rises every day; therefore the sun will rise tomorrow.' While it is conceivable that one day the sun will not rise, the probability of the sun rising is extremely high because of our experience to date.

Conjecture – which is reasoning that involves the formation of conclusions from incomplete evidence.

Argument – which is a course of reasoning aimed at demonstrating a truth or falsehood.

Where deductive reasoning relies solely on logic, inductive reasoning is based on probability and inference.

Whether you are conscious of using abstract reasoning or not, you often employ it in business life and teamworking.

ANALYTICAL/LOGICAL THINKING

He is a true fugitive who flies from reason.

Marcus Aurelius

Analytical and logical thinking requires the use of a methodical step-by-step approach to break down complex problems or processes into their constituent parts. Then you can identify causes and effects, find patterns and analyse problems to arrive at an appropriate solution. This is highly relevant to many of the challenges teamworking presents.

Logical thinking is about using correct reasoning and sound argument. It's not about how you actually argue or reason but about how you ought to reason. It enables you to arrive at your own independent opinions, unbiased and free from bad reasoning.

According to Arm-Chair Logic (Colin Beckley and friends):

> *Logic is not about choice or how to make choices. Being logical cannot tell you which coat to buy or tell you what you ought or ought not to do... It won't tell you what 'good' behaviour is and what 'bad' behaviour is. Being logical is not gender specific. Either sex has the potential to develop and improve their logical techniques.*

Try their logic test at www.think-logically.co.uk/lt.htm

RESOURCE ALLOCATION

Just in terms of allocation of time resources, religion is not very efficient. There's a lot more I could be doing on a Sunday morning.

Bill Gates

Resource allocation is the assignment of resources to tasks in a project. This requires computing a schedule that considers both how to manage limited availability and how to minimize time and cost.

For any team leader, the key resources are usually people, budget, equipment and time. Resource allocation is part of the planning process and is very important where time, money, materials and people are limited.

In the wider sense, resource allocation is a plan for using available resources, for example, human resources, to achieve future goals. It is the process of allocating limited resources among the various tasks. There is the basic allocation decision and there are also contingencies and adjustments to be made as the task or plan rolls out.

Exercise
▶ What tasks should you choose to include in your plan?
▶ What level of resource should each receive and which will receive none?

Resources will always need to be allocated to some items and not to others.

Priorities are important. One priority is to consider which tasks, currently excluded from the plan, will be undertaken if more resources become available. Another priority is just the opposite and is the consideration of which tasks should be sacrificed if the resources are reduced for whatever reason.

RESPONDING TO CHANGE

Life can either be accepted or changed. If it is not accepted, it must be changed. If it cannot be changed, then it must be accepted.

Unknown

The challenges facing teams often demand that they change their approach when it fails to work, when they are running out of time or when an alternative point of view prevails.

Change comes regardless. The only rational response to change is to anticipate, plan for and manage it from whichever direction it comes. Not all change is the same. This current period is marked by examples everywhere of sudden, dramatic, discontinuous change. At other times in history, change has been more gradual and continuous. Change is triggered by internal as well as external factors.

There is a big difference between people saying: 'We are used to change' and actually managing it effectively. At the level of the organization, the capacity to manage change arises from in-built flexibility. Flexibility, speed of response and effectiveness are the three key elements in responding successfully to change.

Flexibility arises in an organization from a variety of factors including:

► open, two-way communication
► effective delegation
► dedication to quality service and customer satisfaction
► adding value rather than just doing the job
► shared understanding of the objectives
► people who feel valued and listened to.

People may be capable of changing but be unwilling to do so.

They may simply not understand how they themselves and/or the organization will benefit from the change and therefore be suspicious and reluctant to change. Communications and motivational issues will have to be addressed in order to shift attitudes towards accepting and being willing to implement the change.

People may be willing to change but unable to do so because they lack the capability to change.

This will often be for reasons not of their own making. They may not have the skills or they may not have the time. Therefore a combination of training and rethinking the job will be necessary for the change to succeed. Where people are unwilling to change and are less than fully capable, a major obstacle to change is in the making.

Willingness and the capability to change are very relevant to successful teamworking.

CREATIVITY

There is nothing in a caterpillar that tells you it's going to be a butterfly

Buckminster Fuller

All children are artists. The problem is how to remain an artist once they grow up.

Pablo Picasso

Many teamwork challenges call for creativity. Unless the task specifically calls for it, this does not mean creativity in the sense of writing a symphony or painting a picture. In this sense, many participants will say that they are not creative but in fact, as is demonstrated below, everyone can learn to express their creativity.

The key is to develop some simple skills. In teambuilding activities, creativity arises where participants are able to see the task in a different way and suggest an alternative solution. Creativity can often come from the failure to solve a problem rather than success. Failure stimulates team members to think harder and to think differently.

There are some familiar phrases that describe this ability: 'think outside the box' or 'push the envelope' or 'come from left field'. All have at their core the idea of seeing the situation in a different and original way. This insight does not belong only to the few.

So is creativity the home of the few or something everyone can do with encouragement?

The best way to get a good idea is to get a lot of ideas.

Linus Pauling

Creativity in the business environment is not about artistic or creative expression. Thinking creatively allows you to make your business stand out from the competition. It's a powerful problem-solving tool rather than change for the sake of change. Most people fear change: they don't necessarily like to be thought of as different, or they don't want to stand out from the crowd.

However, if you can engage creative thinking within your organization on a regular basis, then creative thinking becomes the norm and it is no longer something that stands out.

There are six myths about creativity, according to Robert Epstein. You can read more about creativity in his book *The Big Book of Creativity Games: Quick, Fun Activities for Jumpstarting Innovation* (McGraw Hill, 1995), but here is a summary of the myths:

1 *Creativity is rare.*
   This is not true. The neural processes that underpin creativity are universal. In fact, it's impossible to utter a sentence without them.

2 *Only people with high IQs are creative.*
   While a correlation between intelligence and creativity exists, no particular degree of intelligence has been shown necessary to think creatively.

3 *Creativity can't be studied.*
   Psychology used to be considered beyond the reach of human understanding. Now the study of creativity is recognized in its own right.

4 *Creativity is located in your right brain.*
   No one has yet found a specific neural location for creativity.

5 *Creativity is mysterious.*
   Many aspects of the creative process are now understood.

6 *Creativity can't be learned.*
   Everyone can learn to express greater creativity. The key is to develop some simple skills.

You might like to take this free online test which explores your own creativity competencies: http://mycreativityskills.com/

Epstein goes on to say that creativity emerges in an orderly and predictable way and that such behaviour can be precisely engineered. New ideas come from a combination of previous knowledge, thoughts, experiences and feelings. Failure helps spur the creative processes in predictable ways.

There are four things you can do to help stimulate creative thinking.

1 **Capturing:** Preserve new ideas as they occur. Dictaphone, tape recorder, phone messaging, jotter pad, whichever you use, keep it handy. You never know when a creative moment will hit you.

2 **Challenging:** Failure spurs creativity. If you can't get through the door, try, try, try again. Eventually you'll come up with an answer if the goal is strong enough.

3 **Broadening:** By increasing your knowledge base you add new opportunities on which to build. If you knew only Beethoven, your symphony would probably sound like his. Listen to lots of composers and your own style becomes peppered with them all, producing a style that is inevitably your own.

4 **Surroundings:** Multiple behaviours can be set in motion by multiple or unusual stimuli in the environment. You can accelerate and direct your creative processes by changing our physical and social environments, e.g. where you are and who you sit with.

If you wish to be more creative in your work, try following these tips from Margaret MacKenzie of Entegra Logistics:

▶ Know what it is you want to achieve...
▶ ...but not how you are going to achieve it – live with some uncertainty.
▶ Take an aerial view and look at the whole picture.
▶ Change your assumptions.
▶ Be open by removing the fear and letting your creativity grow.
▶ Use other people to help stimulate and develop ideas.
▶ Learn from your successes as well as from your mistakes.

BIG PICTURE
Details create the big picture.

Sanford I. Weill

While not a business skill or benefit in itself, the ability to see the big picture is an asset in teamworking.

Taking an overview and seeing things in the round is a useful skill to have. Part of this skill is not getting tied down in the details and the other part is a matter of timing. At the start of a task, seeing the big picture will help the team to plan before acting. As stated in the

'Build trust and learn to plan' section of this chapter, too often teams rush into action before taking the time to think things through. Towards the end of task, however, attention is more likely to be focused on the details, with precision coming to the fore. At this late stage, taking time out for a 'helicopter view' – a top down overview of the big picture – may be time wasted.

Certain team-building tasks encourage big picture thinking, and one of the most popular is to set up a large canvas and get each team to paint a portion of the whole. While they work on the pieces individually, they need to bear in mind that their separate square will become one part of a larger whole. Seeing the total picture come together is both physically and symbolically a great experience.

WHICH TEAMWORK SKILLS DO YOU NEED?

You will be an exceptionally gifted team leader if you possess all of these skills. Don't feel in any way inadequate if you lack any of them at this stage in your development. Concentrate on the four key skills of listening, communicating, building trust and planning. These really are essential. Then assess the additional skills you will need and find most useful in your particular role, team and business. With these clear in your mind, you can set out over time to acquire them.

KEYS TO A WINNING TEAM

What teamwork skills do you need most?

- By definition, to be a successful team leader you need to know how to lead, but also how to listen, how to communicate, how to build trust and how to plan.

How to listen:

- Listen as much as you talk.

- Tune in to what the other person is saying with as much focus as you can.

- Take time to practise and develop; it is well worth the effort.

How to communicate:

- Receiving messages is as important as sending them.

- Use a tone of voice that shows attention, concern and courtesy.

- When briefing the team, be clear and natural but above all be prepared.

How to build trust:

- Trust means believing you can depend on each other to reach a common objective.

- By being trusted, you build the relationship with the team with integrity and consistency.

- When they trust you, people can rely on your word.

How to plan:

- Don't act without planning – measure twice, cut once.

- Time spent planning will result in better execution.

- Planning answers the question: 'How do you get there?'

Additional skills:

- In addition to these core skills identify and build additional skills, such as adaptability and creativity.

8

How to develop your team

In this chapter you will learn:
- *that team members have their own needs for development both individually and collectively*
- *what your options and possibilities are for improvement*
- *what role team-building activities can play and if they are effective.*

In developing this book a number of team leaders were asked:

▶ What steps do you take to develop team members?
▶ What kind of training is appropriate?
▶ How do you develop the team as a whole?
▶ Have you used team-building activity sessions?
▶ If so, were they effective and in what ways? And if not effective, why not?

Here is a summary of their responses:

From the Project Director:

People need external training to help them grow but this must arise out of their job itself and their own experience. Otherwise it will be irrelevant to their actual job, role and tasks and thus inappropriate and wasteful. One good team-building activity is the creation of the next year plan for the team or organization as a whole, where it is relatively small.

From the Dancer:

Team members need words of encouragement with a daily class and warm up for practice before every show. They need to work on their skills and to be aware of the need to work together as a team. The better the people, the better the performance will be. The best team members are humble and good at the job.

From the Banker:

I set up new ring binders with a proper development file for each team member and established regular one-on-one sessions to create and monitor personal development plans (PDPs) for each team member. This provided consistency and feedback. Team members needed to understand that their PDP was separate from their core objectives and the needs of the business. They had to meet these business objectives but the PDP was for their own development within the wider organization.

From the RAF Officer:

Identify strengths and weaknesses of individual members. It is important to acknowledge strengths. Too often leaders only concentrate on the weaknesses. This is bad for the morale of the group.

Sometimes individuals need training tailored to them but, where possible, training in team groups helps to create a team spirit.

From the Air Traffic Controller:

Monitor individual performance and identify behaviours that need correcting, or training needs of team members. However, also identify and acknowledge the strengths of your team members. This enhances good practice and improves the morale of the individual whose work is valued and encourages weaker members to try to adopt the same behaviours.

Maximize the team's potential

Nicky Hayes in *Train Your Team Yourself!* (Lisa Hadfield-Law, How To Books, 2002) proposes four different approaches to building a team:

- ▶ interpersonal
- ▶ role based
- ▶ values based
- ▶ task based.

INTERPERSONAL

An interpersonal approach develops high levels of social and personal awareness among team members.

Team members learn how to listen and how to develop more effective communication channels. If they understand each other well enough, they will work together effectively. A culture of trust and confidence will grow out of open discussion about relationships and conflicts.

ROLE BASED

This approach emphasizes role definition as a major task.

The aim is to clarify each individual's role expectations and shared responsibilities towards the other team members. They are encouraged to see themselves from the outside. This makes them aware of their own styles of interaction and helps them learn how to change their style to help the team as a whole and operate more effectively.

VALUES BASED

A values-based approach focuses on a shared understanding between team members.

When everyone in the team holds common values and the team's aims reflect those values, then team members should be able to work together effectively. Team-building activity days are valuable so all can focus on a shared vision.

TASK BASED

This is less about what people are like and more about what they can do.

Here there's a heavy emphasis on the exchange of information among team members with a systematic approach to the task in terms of resources, skills and practical steps.

Most team-building activities use one of these four approaches, if not a mixture.

How to develop yourself

NEW TEAM LEADER EXPERIENCES

What support can you expect when you are first appointed as a new team leader? This can vary greatly from none to (more unusually) a planned programme of development.

> **Exercise**
> For those of you who are already team leaders:
>
> ▶ What was your experience?
> ▶ What tips could you give to others in the same position?
> ▶ Here are some typical experiences of being a first time team leader.

BillBlue wrote on July 2009

> *When I was appointed, I asked my manager if there was any training going to be provided. My request was met with some surprise! The view seemed to be that because I was good at my 'old' job, the assumption was made that I would also be good at this one. I was managing people for the first time and basically had to learn on my feet!*

MelBelle wrote on July 2009:

> *When I first started being a manager I was left to find my own way. My team was restructured and I inherited two members of staff. I asked my boss if there was any training or reading I should do and she said that there was a five-day course but not for a couple of months. Great! It was quite daunting as I am not a natural leader; I don't feel terribly comfortable telling people what to do. My job was stressful enough trying to get everything done without keeping an eye on two other people (one who worked in a different office 200 miles away).*
>
> *In the end I had to just play it by ear. There was a difficult situation around performance and sickness of one of the people which I could have handled differently. Generally though, I think I did OK. My main focus was to be supportive, work with them to find solutions to their problems and have regular one-on-one meetings with each of them to catch up on their projects. I also*

*created projects that you all worked on together as a way of
making us work more like a team.*

*My tip for new team leaders is to think about how you are
managed and use this to understand your own style. Follow your
instincts and get support from other team leaders and your own
manager. HR issues can be difficult to deal with so find someone
that you can talk these through with.*

Both from www.knowhownonprofit.org

HOW TO DEVELOP YOURSELF ON LITTLE OR NO BUDGET

Low-cost ideas for personal development
There are many free or cost effective ways for you to learn and develop.

Here are some examples provided by Fiona Ash on
www.knowhownonprofit.org:

- ▶ being coached or mentored
- ▶ seeking advice from others
- ▶ work shadowing (inside or outside your organization)
- ▶ e-learning
- ▶ internal knowledge sharing events
- ▶ job rotation
- ▶ new assignments and work experience
- ▶ reading books, articles and watching DVDs or online media
- ▶ learning from others who have specialist knowledge
- ▶ starting a peer learning or action learning group.

Reflecting on learning
Reflecting after you have completed a project, an activity or piece of
work can be a great way of developing yourself.

Exercise
Think about:

- ▶ what went well and not so well
- ▶ the reasons behind this
- ▶ what you might do differently next time
- ▶ what you learned from the experience
- ▶ the changes you need to make as a result.

You can do this on your own or with others who were part of
the project or activity.

The key to ensuring that you retain the new knowledge or skill is to make sure you apply it as soon as you get back to work and tell others about it too. Explaining something you have learned to another person is an excellent way of reinforcing that knowledge or skill.

> ### Exercise
> What free or low-cost personal development opportunities have you experienced or developed yourself?

Adapted from Fiona Ash on www.knowhownonprofit.org

UNDERSTAND YOUR AND OTHERS' LEARNING STYLE

According to Fiona Ash, the key to learning most effectively is understanding your learning style. When you understand how you like to learn, you can make the most of your learning opportunities. It will help you choose which type of personal development activity will suit you best and help you make the most of your organization's resources.

Perhaps you have had the experience of trying to learn something simple and have failed to grasp the main point. You may have tried to teach something, only to find that some people were overwhelmed or confused by something quite basic. If this is the case, then you may have experienced a clash of learning styles.

Your learning preferences and your audience's may not have been aligned. When this happens, not only is it frustrating for everyone, the communication process breaks down and learning fails.

When you know your natural learning preference, you can start to expand the way you learn, so that you can learn in other ways and not just in your preferred style. By understanding learning styles, you can learn to create an environment where everyone can learn from you, not just those who use your preferred style.

Everyone has a different preferred way of experiencing and perceiving the world and this has an effect on the way you learn:

- ▶ some people like theory
- ▶ some prefer the details
- ▶ some need to see the big picture
- ▶ others learn by doing.

148

Some people learn better through seeing, some by hearing, others by touching and so on.

This is sometimes referred to as 'VAK' learning styles standing for visual, auditory and kinaesthetic. These three styles are associated with the following activities:

Learning style	Description
Visual	seeing and reading
Auditory	listening and speaking
Kinaesthetic	touching and doing

N.B. Kinaesthetic style is also referred to as 'Physical' or 'Tactile'.

For a free self-test on your learning preference, go to: www.businessballs.com/vaklearningstylestest.htm

Everyone has their preferences and it's important to recognize that other people learn in different ways, and so something you find hard to learn they may find easy and vice versa.

Adapted from Fiona Ash on:
www.knowhownonprofit.org/people/your-development/your-learning-development/
learningopps

THE FIVE DYSFUNCTIONS OF A TEAM: A LEADERSHIP FABLE

To see what happens when the team isn't working, Patrick Lencioni's book *The Five Dysfunctions of a Team: A Leadership Fable, (2002)* Jossey-Bass has a good example.

The five dysfunctions around which Lencioni builds his book are:

- ▶ absence of trust
- ▶ fear of conflict
- ▶ lack of commitment
- ▶ avoidance of accountability
- ▶ inattention to results.

The story is told as a fable whose heroine is the CEO of a struggling Silicon Valley firm. She is hired to bring together a dysfunctional executive staff to work as a team in a company that just two years earlier had looked promising. She takes control of the executive committee and helps its members succeed as a team.

'Building a cohesive team is not complicated,' declares Lencioni. Departing from the dry, theoretical writing of many management books, he presents his case in the context of a fictional organization which helps him succeed in communicating his ideas.

The scenarios are recognizable and can be applied anywhere teamwork is involved, whether it is a multinational company or a small department within a larger organization. At the end of the story, the main points are summarized, and clearly written suggestions and exercises are offered to help bring about change. This is a great book is for anyone who is a member of a team that needs improvement.

Adapted from Bellinda Wise's review, (April 15, 2002) in the Library Journal of Nassau Community Call. Lib. Garden City, NY

Essentially, Lencioni's model of a dysfunctional team is the mirror image of a successfully functioning team. Here you would hope to find in abundance trust, commitment, accountability, attention to results and, if not the absence of conflict, then the capacity to accept and deal with it.

This is a good model to hold in your mind before continuing.

Team-building activities

From the Banker:

> *It can be good to take a step back, e.g. a formal two-day residential course, or it can be more informal. In a sense, the activities themselves don't matter, it's the experience of being together and bonding as a team.*

You need to set individual targets but do it within the team culture of helping each other. Internal politics can disrupt otherwise good relations within the team.

From the RAF Officer:

> *I found team-building activities entertaining but not necessarily any more use than having a social occasion. However, I have*

spent nearly all of my working life in teams, starting in the RAF where the training was almost wholly concentrated on this aspect. I suspect that it is useful for people at the beginning of their careers when they don't have much experience of the goal-oriented behaviour of teams.

One way to develop your team is by conducting team-building activities. These are very popular today and are usually delivered by external companies. Here are some recommendations:

▶ For new teams, and changing teams in particular, well-chosen team-building activities can help bond the team together.
▶ When the team is performing well, an event can be seen as a reward.
▶ When the team is performing badly, an event can be a diagnostic and a corrective.

Of course, a team-building event does mean taking half a day or even a whole day out from the office and regular business activities. While the benefits on offer in terms of improved teamworking are significant, there will often be team members who think they are too busy to take part and who believe it will simply add to the pressure they are already under. While no one should be compelled to take part against their will, you should use your powers of persuasion to convince them that the positives outweigh the negatives and that the time will be well invested. Check with them after the event to see if they have changed their opinion. The chances are they will be feeling more positive about the team and about themselves.

FUN VERSUS LEARNING

While of course an event can be pure fun and nothing else, team-building activities can be much more than just fun, giving rise to real business benefits when planned and executed properly.

What starts out as a simple 'fun day' can evolve into something different. A common remark is: 'We came to have fun but found there was more to it.' Activities are subtle and can change shape during the course of the day. You need to be clear about the objectives.

You can combine business content with activities. One approach is to devise business scenarios that take place outdoors. For example, key information on which the team has to base a presentation is placed to be discovered at the foot of an abseil.

THE TEAM-BUILDING EVENT

An event is likely to be a collection of activities lasting about half a day to a complete day. The location will usually be outside, though the activities can take place inside. For the event example detailed below, an open space is needed, typically about the size of a football pitch like a lawn at a hotel or a field at a sports or leisure centre or school. The event organizers will have laid out everything in advance earlier in the day. Emphasis is laid upon the safety of participants at all times and each activity is supervised by an instructor or facilitator.

Team-building event example

In the example described here, the event took place over most of a day outside on the playing field area of a health club. There were four groups of six to eight participants of mixed gender and ages, shapes and sizes. In this case, leaders have not been chosen in advance. The duration of the event meant there was plenty of time to discuss each activity with the facilitator in order to draw out the lessons that had been learned.

In total, there were eight activities for the teams to complete during the course of the day, plus a big finale event to round things off in spectacular fashion and send people home on a high with something truly memorable. Examples of the activities were:

▶ bridge building: where the team has to cross a gap using the resources of two poles and a plank
▶ herding sheep: where a blindfolded 'sheep' finds the way to the pen following a series of non-verbal messages from the 'shepherd'
▶ an imaginary minefield: where the safe route through a grid is concealed and the team must one by one attempt to find a safe route through
▶ a hazardous chemical event: where one large tube of chemical has to be decanted into two smaller tubes in exact units.

Examples courtesy of Progressive Resources – The Teambuilding Company at
www.teambuilding.co.uk

These are all events that comprise a specific challenge within a limited time with limited resources. This type of activity best lends itself to facilitation.

Each of the four groups spent 20 to 30 minutes on each activity. Following each activity there was a discussion with the facilitator. This can be long or short but can often last as long as the activity itself. Here is where the all-important connection can be made with business benefits and where the transfer of learning to the workplace can be discussed.

What has taken place here?
Within the space of a few hours, a day out of the office has certainly included fun and social bonding. But there can be much more to team building than this. Everyone has contributed because of the wide range of skills involved. Every challenge plays a part in the final solution. No individual team member can achieve a result by working alone. Every challenge has more than one route to the solution, drawing on an alternative discipline. The participants leave at the end of the day with satisfaction and a genuine sense of achievement.

Bridge building
Now let's look at one specific task in detail. Here's the scenario:

A raging river has washed away a bridge that you desperately need to cross. All that's left are some pillars protruding from the raging torrent, and all you have to hand are two poles that can be used a number of times and a plank that once placed with weight put onto it, must remain fixed. The task is to transfer the team across the watery hazard to safety.

KEY SKILLS
Consider what skills and disciplines are involved in completing this task.

- ▶ Communication: listening carefully and verbalizing effectively.
- ▶ Leadership: making decisions and taking control of the task.
- ▶ Planning: agreeing a plan as a team and following it through.
- ▶ Teamwork: working effectively together as a team.
- ▶ Building trust: requiring significant support from the team.
- ▶ Assertiveness: getting your ideas across to the team.
- ▶ Adaptability: adapting the plan as the task requires.
- ▶ Abstract reasoning: analysing a problem and coming up with a solution.

- ▶ Resource allocation: thinking about which resources to use when.
- ▶ Change management: considering that the plan may have to change.

This activity has wide ranging relevance to business:

- ▶ Communication: the ability to communicate, both verbally and through good listening skills, is important throughout all levels of an organization.
- ▶ Leadership: having someone who takes decisions and leads from the front after listening to the team's input.
- ▶ Planning: having a plan is vital to success. Would you start a new business venture without having a plan to make it succeed?
- ▶ Teamwork: the combination of mental and physical aspects of the activity demonstrates that team members contribute according to their abilities. They will need help from other team members to complete the task. This mirrors the interrelationships seen between different departments within an organization.
- ▶ Trust: trust is the bedrock of all team activity. Without trust the team cannot function. With trust the team can achieve a shared objective.
- ▶ Resource allocation: in business, it is unlikely you would sacrifice your most valuable resource at the start of your business venture, but rather you would hold it in reserve until it could be used most effectively.
- ▶ Change management: the ability and capability to adapt and to manage change are also important considerations. It is unlikely that you would stick to a business plan that is fundamentally flawed. You would change it in order to make it work.

By the end there is a real sense of achievement in a controlled and safe environment with a skilful facilitator where every team member has had the opportunity to learn more about themselves and their fellow team members.

FACILITATION
The purpose of the facilitator is first to draw out of the event the lessons learned about the event itself, and then to invite the team

members to make the connection to their behaviour at work. The degree to which this is successful will determine the relevance of team-building events to life back in the workplace.

Two approaches are possible when an organization commissions an event – one approach is closed, the other is open.

1 *Closed: 'What do you want to get out of it?'*
   When planning a team-building event, you may wish the event to focus on specific skills so team members get something back from the event such as learning for leadership or communication. They will want to be able to ask afterwards: 'Where was the leadership or communication?' and 'What specific lessons were learned in these areas?' By defining the inputs and outputs in advance, you get what you've asked for, but nothing more.

2 *Open: 'No fixed agenda'*
   The alternative approach is where you and your team members go into the event with an open mind and without seeking fixed objectives or outcomes. You want to see what emerges. These will be the issues that really matter to the team. These will often be broader and deeper than the results of the first approach. Here you get what you haven't asked for but it may be much more interesting!

By the very nature of your role as a team leader, you may tend to look for goals and objectives and at first will tend towards the more closed approach. However, if you can trust the team and the event organizers to adopt the open approach – and it is a big act of trust – then the rewards can be much greater.

Which is the more risky? You'd think it would be the open approach but in fact there are times when there is more risk in the first approach. This is when your team members have not been consulted and have not bought into the objectives. In the open approach, this cannot be the case by definition.

MOTIVATION

At its most basic form, motivation arises from the fact that the company allows the event to happen and spends money on doing it. It can be a simple 'thank you' day from the company. It sends the message: 'You are successful enough for your company to do this for you.' This makes people feel valued.

Winning is another aspect of motivation. Winning is important and team members need to feel they have met the challenge and triumphed. The challenge needs to be demanding but not out of reach. Winning is different from competition. In the most rewarding events, everyone goes home feeling they have won.

Scores and fun prizes are a means of tracking progress and rewarding achievement. Fun prizes can be sweets or chocolates for the winning team, i.e. nothing that will increase competitiveness. It's recognition rather than reward.

A well-performing team is very different from a team with a problem. While both can benefit from team-building events, they require different approaches. A team that is performing well needs celebrating and rewarding to keep it on an upward spiral. A team with serious issues needs to bring these out to prevent the team sliding into a downward spiral.

COMPETITION AND NON-COMPETITIVE TEAM BUILDING

One of the problems with the traditional team-building event format is that it is, by its very nature, divisive. A selection of activities is laid on and the group is divided into teams to have a go at each activity. An example might be a group of 20 divided into four teams of five to try archery, laser shooting, quad bikes or dune buggies.

Not only does this isolate people into teams, which may even be separated over the course of the event, but often teams are encouraged to compete against each other so that a winning team can be announced at the end of the event. Some argue that this is contrary to the aims of team building. Extreme activities such as abseiling and bungee jumping are even more divisive. Rather than building a team, they separate a team into those who are afraid and those who are not.

Depending on the type of culture you and your organization wish to encourage, you may choose a highly competitive form of activity, for example, for a sales team who compete against each other every day at work. Alternatively you may opt for a less competitive and more co-operative approach. Here are some examples of how that can work.

One solution is to change the members of the teams at each rotation, but this can be time consuming and upset the equilibrium. Another solution often employed is to play down the competition in the events and not to have winners announced at the end. However, humans are naturally competitive creatures and even if the organizer is not comparing scores you can be assured that the participants will.

There has been a growth in non-competitive team-building programmes. These use one task which the whole team involves itself in together. Thus individuals are not separated from each other and the competition is between the team and the task and not between sub-teams.

One of the most popular of these, mentioned earlier, is the task where teams work on smaller paintings which are put together in the end to make one big picture. Communication between all participants is essential so that the cumulative result achieves some sort of congruence with the individual pictures. The final painting can be kept by the participants to remind them of the activity.

Insight

There are various other options available including Community Team-Building in which teams take on a community project, for example, renovating a building or transforming wasteland into a garden. Another example is that of a team that builds an enclosure at a wildlife park for young tigers. The possibilities for projects of this nature are limitless.

In the majority of cases, the essential requirement of team-building events is that the participants have fun, and in such cases the traditional round robin activity format may be appropriate.

Event ingredients

What are the essential elements of a team-building event? Let's use the bridge building example.

The bridge building activity described how team members are challenged to build a bridge across an imaginary ravine using two poles and one planks.

This task involves:

▶ leadership – whether named (explicit) or not (implicit)
▶ limited time

- limited resources
- usually a degree of (appropriate) physical contact
- a perception of risk (although in reality the physical risk is actually very, very small.)
- team building dos and don'ts
- boundaries and ground rules.

You have to be careful not to offend people. Some events can be corny and participants don't like that. Taking part will make them feel embarrassed. Events which rely on humour cannot be relied on to appeal to everyone and need to be treated with care. The best events give the illusion of risk without actually putting anyone at risk. You have to remember that the average person does not take physical risks on a daily basis. Few of us are mountaineers or Formula One racing drivers. Participants should not be scared, but should have their boundaries gently pushed. They do need to be challenged because challenges force people to think on their feet in the face of consequences.

Do not seek to have events happen as you want them to but instead want them to happen as they do happen and your life will go well.

Epictetus (Greek Stoic philosopher, AD 55 – c.135)

Choosing an event, what to consider and what questions to ask
Consider:

- objectives
- length
- numbers
- fun or learning
- challenges
- constraints.

Organizing events with maximum appeal
One of the greatest challenges for the event organizer is to arrange a variety of activities that will appeal to everyone in the team. Obviously it is impossible to choose activities that all will like but it is important to have variety so that everyone will have something to enjoy. The most common format for outdoor participation events is

to have a range of activities. A group of 30 might be divided into five teams to attempt six different activities.

There is a general feeling that shooting and motorized activities are enjoyed more by men than by women. This is by no means a rule and there are always exceptions, but if an event is dominated by this sort of activity some people will enjoy it more than others.

Choosing the activities wisely will help; for example, archery tends to be enjoyed by more people than clay pigeon shooting because some people find the noise and kickback of the shotgun too violent.

The most important thing is to ensure that the organizers stress that the event is run on a 'challenge by choice' basis. If someone decides that they do not want to do something then they should not be forced to participate or be humiliated. This is the last thing that should happen on a team-building day.

One of the most popular types of event is the Treasure Hunt. These are popular because they are not overly physically demanding and do not obviously appeal to either sex more than the other. Command challenges can be built into the format and events can be tailored to an organization's particular needs.

What to consider
To start everyone in a fresh state of mind, choose a country house hotel with access to good walking territory and have a team-building walk after breakfast. Often teams start an event after a large breakfast, having not left the centrally heated environment of the hotel building – not the best way to get you going in the morning.

You might arrange a light-hearted aerobic session before an event – nothing too strenuous, primarily fun but out in the open and designed to get the blood flowing to the brain. Light stretching exercises are an excellent way to start an event and the fun is a good ice breaker.

Every activity provided by an event company should have a unique Risk Assessment. A Risk Assessment ensures that potential dangers have been considered and steps taken to minimize the risk. Activities are then classified as low, medium and high risk. You may decide to avoid high risk activities on your event.

Now that you have been given a detailed description of team-building events, it's time to ask the critical question: do team-building days really help teams to work together?

Does team building work?

Do team-building days such as white water rafting or assault courses really help teams to work together?

Dawn Smith on the Training Zone website spoke to a wide range of providers and users of team-building activities. Here are some examples of the comments she collected.

According to Graham O'Connell of the National School of Government:

> *The key with team building, as with any event, is to be clear about the purpose and then design the event to meet that purpose. Adventurous activities can be an engaging part of the mix, but I do think that more often than not they are used as a form of entertainment or reward or as a shared challenge in the vague hope this will bring people together (which it may or may not).*

According to John Wright at Symbiosis Consulting, a reward is fine but it's not team building:

> *Away days and activities, even in isolation, can be great for rewarding people who have worked hard. If activities are well organized, safe and appropriately challenging I am sure that people will bond together faster than in most office environments. However, let's not get carried away with this.*

An outdoor activity away day is unlikely to be a life changing experience or long-term performance boost on its own.

Dawn Smith argues that for a long-term, positive effect on the way a team works together, activities have to be used appropriately, in the context of a team development initiative and then related back to the work environment.

For John Wright that means:

A blended programme of relevant theory, outdoor and indoor action and team based problem-solving, excellent facilitation to help participants draw parallels with their work and life experience, setting personal and team goals to take learning back to work/life.

OBJECTIVES

Ken Minor, Director of Leadership Resources, uses an integrated approach with outdoor and indoor team exercises combined with classroom work.

Teams need to understand their roles and what they need to do in order to achieve their objectives, for example, communicate freely, and you can't learn that sitting round a table.

Kathleen Harrison-Carroll at Katalan, the experiential learning specialists, says:

It's important for individuals to be able to immediately apply what they have learned. There's a huge difference between knowing a thing and being able to use that knowledge.

Karen Stone at R&A Consultancy describes this transition from thinking to doing:

By putting delegates in live leadership/teaming situations, they get to explore what works and what gets in the way of success. Having them feel, see and understand the impact of their behaviour, they can then put in place actions to develop what they've learned. This means they return to the business with a set of behaviours that they need to do in order to achieve their desired outcomes.

BREAKING DOWN BARRIERS

Taking part in activities can be a great leveller. Ken Minor adds:

> *Outdoor activities can take away the status and hierarchy. When you are out on the moors without a mobile signal everyone is focused as a team on what they are being asked to do.*

According to Alan Hunt, MD of team building company Sandstone, if everyone is required to pursue just one or two physical activities like abseiling or quad biking, this can be detrimental to team building.

> *When you have just one activity, a third of the group will love it, a third won't mind doing it and a third will think it's their idea of hell. The team then splits. The third that hated doing it bonds together and the two thirds who love it or don't mind doing it bond together. So you have two cliques.*

To counteract this tendency, Sandstone activities are designed so teams work towards a goal to achieve that requires a number of different skills. For example, in the activity called 'Cube', teams must complete various tasks, ranging from intellectual conundrums to racing in giant caterpillar tracks, in order to earn pieces of a giant cube that they are assembling.

Alan Hunt says:

> *None of the tasks are compulsory and the focus is on the team processes required to tackle the activity successfully. There are too many tasks to do them all, so teams have to prioritize. At the debrief, you can focus on the parallels of the processes in the workplace.*

LONG-TERM IMPACT AND EVALUATION

Alan Hunt stresses that team building can have a long lasting impact through the changes they bring about in methodology.

> *A team-building event can highlight ways in which the team's methodology can be improved. If you ask them to do something unfamiliar, you take away their biggest crutch which is*

experience. Then you can expose good and bad methodology in teams and look at how that can be improved and applied back to the workplace.

All agree that measuring the impact of team-building events on the business is difficult. At Sandstone, evaluation focuses on three areas:

- ▶ the original key performance indicators (KPIs) of the business
- ▶ response from participants (i.e. basically asking participants)
- ▶ an intermediate measure to determine how well the purpose of the event has been achieved.

Says Alan Hunt:

It comes back to what you want out of the event in the first place.

Adapted from Dawn Smith, *Team-Building: What Difference Does it Make?*
(Training Zone, 2007) www.trainingzone.co.uk/item/174435

KEYS TO A WINNING TEAM

Maximizing the team's potential:

- The best people give the best performance and are the most humble.

- External training must arise out of the job itself.

How to develop your learning styles:

- By understanding your personal learning style you will learn more effectively.

- Everyone has a different learning style which affects the way they learn; some people like theory; some details; some need to see the big picture; others learn by doing.

- Development options are available that do not require a big budget, e.g. e-learning, internal knowledge sharing events or job rotation.

Team-building activities:

- Consider team building to develop your team using an external company.

- For new and changing teams, team-building activities can bond the team together.

- When the team is performing well, an event can be seen as a reward.

- When the team is performing badly, an event can be a diagnostic and corrective.

Possible downsides to team-building activities

Just fun with no learning?

- Activity experiences may fail to transfer to the workplace.

- Members' preferences for activities may be divisive – not all can like the same things.

Do team-building activities work?

- Evaluate activities for short-term and longer term effects on performance back at work.

9

How to find the right way to talk to your team

In this chapter you will learn:
- *how to communicate best with your team members*
- *how to manage the team's time in an efficient manner*
- *the best ways to reach and communicate decisions.*

When is a meeting the most useful means of communicating with your team members? How often should they be held? How necessary are meetings, really? When are they a good use of time and when not? Does the whole team need to be there and does everyone need to be there all time? It's no secret how much time can be wasted in unnecessary or irrelevant meetings.

What about written communication – mainly by e-mail. How do you get the message across most effectively and by what means? Without the body language, does the message get lost? How do you know you've conveyed the right tone when you're not there when the recipient reads it?

And what is the value of one-on-one talks with your team members? Some members find it hard to speak out in a meeting. Make an effort for them and be a good listener. Although it may be time consuming, ask yourself if it is worth the investment.

What's the best way to get the message across?

During the research for *Create a Winning Team*, we asked a selection of team leaders: 'What methods do you find most useful to communicate with team members?' and 'What is your view of meetings?'

From the Banker:

Getting together is good for morale so meetings are generally a good idea. It's the one time everyone is there so there's the opportunity to get across common messages to all team members at the same time and get their comments too. The frequency varies, typically one per month but it all depends on circumstances. You can certainly have too many. A good meeting needs pre-planning.

E-mail is good for communicating too, but for recognition and direct feedback one-on-one sessions are best because they create an individual relationship. When giving feedback I always try to find something positive to comment on and avoid negative feedback as far as possible as it just alienates people. Basically teamwork is all about communication. It's the most important aspect.

Written communication is now most often by e-mail. Never send an e-mail in anger – always sleep on it first. Use different styles for different modes. Fully written reports or memos are different from e-mails which themselves differ from texts or tweets.

From the Lead Artist:

As a lead artist, I have a daily meeting with the team on what we are all doing that day; who's doing what and so on. So everyone knows what is going on and doesn't need to interrupt and ask unnecessary questions later. The meeting lasts as long as it takes – five minutes or fifty. Don't allow one hour or a fixed time every time because you won't always need it.

From the Dancer:

The dance captain who's our team leader organizes rehearsals. It helps when they have good time management and call the right people – that's just the people involved in a particular scene so you don't have people hanging about unnecessarily. It's important they stick to the plan made and the rehearsal times. Where possible, an e-mail the night before with the schedule is really helpful.

From the Air Traffic Controller:

Verbal communication is best when the discussion only involves one or two team members, but e-mail or written communication is important when a lot of people need to have the same information communicated and avoids the need to call a large meeting.

How to hold successful meetings and brief the team

WHEN TO HOLD A MEETING

You should hold meetings regularly for consistency, but the frequency should vary with the type and nature of the business. The meeting could be once a day for ten minutes for a project team or once a month for an hour for a department. Don't make meetings a fixed length and always have an agenda. Some colleagues will even refuse to attend any meetings that do not have an agenda. Circulate material in advance to receive fresh input at the meeting.

From the Project Director:

I'm in favour of meetings if the right people attend and the agenda is right too. In the office you meet regularly and separately with Communications, Development and Programming and we have one large monthly meeting for all seven staff. We circulate articles for discussion in advance or someone presents a new subject to inject fresh input and content into the proceedings.

From the RAF Officer:

A lot of meetings waste an inordinate amount of time because people only start thinking about the subject during the meeting and a lot of waffle ensues. The purpose of an agenda is to plan what is going to be discussed but if it is sent out prior to the meeting, then people can think about the items in advance of the meeting.

This can be helped by the team leader having discussions with critical people who will attend the meeting. No conclusions need be drawn at this stage but team members should be provoked into thinking about the subject. That way the meeting is about the conclusions members have come to and not their initial thoughts. The meeting can then progress by discussing the relative merits of each person's ideas.

HOW TO CONDUCT MEETINGS

Meetings are like a stage performance. You, as team leader, are the producer. As a result you have to prepare yourself in advance as follows:

Set the stage:

- ▶ Give advance warning of the date.
- ▶ Remind everyone again 48 hours before the meeting.
- ▶ Organize the seating – options can be in a horseshoe or semi-circle, or sitting round a table.
- ▶ Minimize interruptions.

Prepare your script:

- ▶ Study the support material and put it into your own words.
- ▶ Group your points, for example:
    - ▷ Past: Review past performance
    - ▷ Present: Discuss what's happening at present
    - ▷ Future: Plan future tactics.
- ▶ Make the information relevant. Consider the needs of your team, for example:
    - ▷ How much do they already know?
    - ▷ How much will they be involved?
    - ▷ How can you motivate them?
- ▶ Anticipate questions.
- ▶ Plan the length of time the meeting will run, e.g. 45 minutes.
- ▶ Get your presentation aids organized.

Keep control of meetings:

- ▶ Resist any distractions.
- ▶ Remind your team of the time restrictions.
- ▶ Be assertive.
- ▶ Keep the attendees motivated.
- ▶ Encourage pride in the company and its products or services.
- ▶ Keep the momentum going and use interim and final summaries. (For more details see the 'Summaries' section later in this chapter.)

RUNNING YOUR MEETINGS

Keeping control of meetings – managing time and managing people – is probably one of the biggest problems you face as a team leader. Time has a nasty habit of running out on you before you've covered the agenda. Add to that the various characters in the team who seem to conspire to make things difficult for you, and you can begin to feel that you'll never run a successful meeting. Here are some descriptions of typical characters in a team and a few tips to help you handle them.

Team characteristics

The **bulldog** – aggressive, inclined to argue, but often knowledgeable. Try not to sit directly opposite the bulldog but have them on your immediate left in a non-confrontational position.

The **horse** – willing, dependable, keen, often knowledgeable and likes to show it; too quick with answers and often no one else gets a turn. Take up their points and ask others what they think.

The **fox** – devious, determined to undermine your leadership. Likes to pick a topic they know you are weak on and display their own knowledge to your disadvantage. Be honest. Say 'I'm afraid that's not one of my strong points, would someone else like to pick up this topic?'

The **monkey** – disruptive, know-it-all, often the office clown. Be careful how you handle the monkey, they are often very popular. Use this to your advantage; show you are human and enjoy the joke but bring the conversation back on course.

The **hedgehog** – prickly, unreceptive to change, unwilling to participate and not inclined to be helpful. They have ability and experience, however, so try to involve them even if they are negative.

The **giraffe** – lofty, superior and above-it-all. Observers by nature. Treat them with respect and encourage them to contribute by asking a direct question. Don't pick a fight with them or they may cease to participate.

The **hippo** – loses interest and may even doze off in meetings. Don't allow this to happen. Check that they are still with you by speaking to them by name and drawing them into the proceedings.

The **wide-mouthed frog** – talks about anything except the topic in hand. Be assertive but tactful and refocus the issue. Use time as a valid reason for ending their chit-chat.

The **gazelle** – young, new or part-time. Not necessarily shy. It is important that you involve them but don't ask them questions until you are confident they can answer correctly. Embarrassing them will scare them off.

Originally adapted from: The Industrial Society
(now Capita Learning and Development)

Exercise
▶ Do you recognize any of these characters in your own team?
▶ Are you confident you know how best to relate to them?
▶ Is there someone you find particularly difficult to handle?

Questioning techniques
There are a variety of questioning techniques that can be used in meetings. For example:

▶ Open: Information must be given in return. They are often directional and begin with How, Where, When, What, Who and Why? These get everyone involved.
▶ Overhead: These questions are intended to make people focus attention on the subject in hand, e.g. 'OK, how can you relate this information to our area?'
▶ Direct: Questions directed at an individual by using their name or direct eye contact.
▶ Re-direct: Same questions directed at another individual to elicit a different response.

▶ Relay: These questions come in useful if you want to avoid influencing the team with your opinion or if you don't know the answer, e.g. 'That's a good question, John. What do you think, Mary?'

Summaries

Time is your greatest weapon, not your enemy. Summaries have a valuable role to play in meetings. They help you control your team member audience and your time.

There are two types of summary, interim and final.

Interim summaries are used to indicate progress or lack of it and:

▶ refocus off-track discussion
▶ tie-up and move forward
▶ highlight important points
▶ clarify misunderstandings.

Final summaries are used to close the proceedings and:

▶ establish the team's conclusions and the points of action arising
▶ allow everyone to leave with a sense of achievement and purpose.

Effective presentation

Public speaking is in the top ten of most people's list things most feared. There are several simple ways to make things easier for yourself when heading up a meeting:

VISUAL AIDS

▶ Plan them.
▶ Keep them simple.
▶ Give the audience time to digest the information.
▶ Limit the number of visual aids you use or they become confusing.
▶ Talk the audience through them and allow for discussion.
▶ Make sure they are visible.

ATTENTION SPAN

The length of your meeting will depend entirely on the subject matter, but bear in mind that most people's attention span rarely exceeds 20 minutes.

This does not mean that you should aim to have the meeting completed in 20 minutes but be prepared to use techniques to maintain your audience's interest, such as:

- ▶ speak clearly
- ▶ encourage discussion
- ▶ ask questions
- ▶ be enthusiastic
- ▶ pause
- ▶ smile
- ▶ use summaries
- ▶ use eye contact
- ▶ control discussion
- ▶ avoid barriers
- ▶ use visual aids
- ▶ avoid jargon.

DEALING WITH NERVES

Nerves never go away completely. They are nature's way of getting you 'psyched up' to meet challenges! The way to tackle nerves is to make sure you have done all the preparation you can before the event. An effective and well run meeting will win the respect of all your team members.

You can see that half the battle lies in getting the groundwork done properly. So always get yourself organized by:

- ▶ reading and understanding your material well in advance of the meeting
- ▶ considering your team and what can they gain from the experience.

How to brief the team
When briefing team members be:

- ▶ prepared
- ▶ clear
- ▶ simple
- ▶ natural.

When you are in 'transmit' mode, to be sure your message gets across to your team members you should:

- ► think before speaking – know what you want to say by making time to think before you speak
- ► watch the timing – decide when and where the right time to say it is
- ► choose the right style – judge how best to say it, e.g. assertively, in a roundabout way, indirectly
- ► maintain eye contact – establish regular eye contact with your audience
- ► keep it simple – avoid saying more than is needed
- ► speak clearly – some people may have difficulty hearing but be embarrassed to say so
- ► use examples – use specific examples to get across complex ideas
- ► use repetition – repeat important points to drive the message home
- ► check response regularly
- ► monitor your team members' responses for signs of confusion or acceptance
- ► use appropriate language – speak in a form the receiver understands without talking down … or up!
- ► match words and body language – don't say sorry through gritted teeth!
- ► be flexible – be prepared to change what you say and the order you say it.

When you are in 'receive' mode to be sure you receive your team members' messages clearly:

- ► clear the mind – rid your mind of all unnecessary 'baggage'; this is made up of all the thoughts and feelings you carry around which are not relevant to the current task
- ► maintain eye contact – establish regular eye contact with the speaker
- ► do not interrupt – allow the speaker to finish without rushing them or finishing their sentences yourself
- ► listen actively – concentrate on what is being said, not on what you want to say next; make some sign of agreement now and then to show you're listening such as a nod, or a brief comment

- ▶ watch other's body language – be aware of the speaker's body language by noticing their posture and facial expressions which often speak louder than their words themselves
- ▶ watch your body language – be aware of your own body language too; are you really listening or are you bored or impatient? It will show on your face or in your gestures, however hard you try to hide it or by fidgeting, finger-tapping or playing with a pencil
- ▶ ask open-ended questions – encourage the speaker to talk more freely by asking open-ended questions; for example, not 'Did you …?' but 'What did you think of …?'
- ▶ check for understanding – check with the speaker if you are not sure what was said; good listeners are not afraid to ask questions when they do not understand
- ▶ listen for the feelings behind the words – do not concentrate just on what is spoken but be aware of all the non-verbal signals too
- ▶ put aside prejudices and assumptions – these cloud your perception so you do not hear clearly what is being said
- ▶ do not get upset – hearing something with which you disagree makes it all too easy to switch off or get angry; when you start making judgements or planning your counterattack, you have stopped receiving
- ▶ take notes as needed – if someone sees you writing things down, they know you are paying attention; it shows you take them seriously
- ▶ summarize – summarize what's been said in your own words at the end; confirm with the speaker that they agree; this prevents misunderstandings which can undermine your relationships later.

Insight

Meetings don't have to be a set length but should only last as long as they need to. You'll seldom be criticized for holding short meetings!

How to write effective e-mails

You and your team members probably receive dozens, and in some cases hundreds, of e-mails every day. E-mails that are over long, unclear, too big or just rambling, waste everyone's time and disk space. But used sensibly, e-mails will save you time and help you be an effective communicator.

When you write e-mails that are focused, meaningful and to the point you make it easier for team members to respond promptly and helpfully. Making sure they receive the information they need – but not more than they need – sets an example for effective communication for the team as a whole. Being able to write effective e-mails is an extremely useful skill that will enable you to communicate more productively with team members and receive a better response.

How do you write an e-mail so it not only gets read but also responded to? You're aiming for an e-mail that will be read and be understood rather than ignored; an e-mail that does not irritate the reader and that does not take up too much of their time.

Consider the sender and the receiver. They have very different perspectives. Typically the sender lacks an understanding of who the receiver is and the pressures they are under. The receiver is probably sent lots of e-mail, is regularly asked questions and for favours, doesn't have much free time but doesn't mind helping if it doesn't take very long.

The sender on the other hand will tend to regard their e-mail as unique and that they are the first to ask the question or for the favour. They will take time to write a long and, in their eyes, perfect e-mail. The sender wants to tell a long tale so the receiver can understand their point of view.

Given such different points of view, receivers should not be surprised to get the e-mail they do and senders should not be astonished their e-mails are not responded to more eagerly.

For the receiver faced with an inbox full of e-mail after, say, a holiday, there is a tendency to answer e-mails that are the fastest to answer, i.e. ones that require the least work or thought. Opening a very long e-mail, they may just close it or return to it later when they have more time.

Therefore, to be an effective communicator it is important to be aware of and sensitive to the receiver's point of view. Doing so will make it more likely that your e-mail will be opened and responded to promptly.

Follow these e-mail best practices to become a great communicator:

1 *Decide on the outcome you desire*
   While you probably know more or less what you want to say, you may not always take the time to think it through clearly. This can make the e-mail unclear or hard to follow. So you need to decide on the outcome you desire, or else your thoughts can be disorganized and you may end up confusing the receiver.

Consider these four types of e-mail:

- *No reply necessary* – The e-mail is simply giving information.
- *Reply needed* – You need something from the receiver in the form of advice or questions to be answered.
- *Continuing dialogue – An open-ended conversation* that keeps communication lines open with some future result in mind.
- *Action e-mail* – Some action is required from the receiver, not just a reply, e.g. an instruction or invitation to attend a meeting.

Which type do you send most? And what do you expect back?

When you are focused and your intention is clear, your e-mails will reflect this and, as a result, you will be more likely to get your desired outcome.

Often receivers only read part way through a long message and click on 'Reply' as soon as they have something to contribute and without reading further. Help the receiver to prioritize by being clear about what you want them to do after reading your message.

For example, is it to:

- answer a simple 'yes' or 'no' question?
- help you solve a problem?
- listen to you and give advice where appropriate?
- file your report in case the information is needed at a later date?

2 *Use the subject line to attract attention*
   Readers see the subject line first. Remember that, of course, it's not the only one in their mailbox. So it's important to come up

with an accurate subject line that defines the content and attracts the reader's attention. It will make the difference between them opening, filing or deleting your e-mail.

3 *Get to the point*

Quickly get to the point in as few words as possible. Readers want to know what you want from them without wading through long introductions or unnecessary details. When action is needed, make it clear what that action is. And if no action or reply is expected, then say so clearly.

4 *Keep your message short and simple*

When you send a long e-mail asking for something from the receiver, you are actually saying 'I do not respect your time.' Show you value their time by making your e-mail short and simple. With the minimum of words, say why you are e-mailing. Brief doesn't mean boring and you can be creative with your wording, adding a dash of personality where you see fit, but still remaining brief.

There's a tendency to say too much in an e-mail. People think they have to go into all the details so the receiver can understand the whole picture. Most times the reality is that they are not really that interested. Stick to the facts and avoid the temptation to over elaborate.

5 *Think before you click 'Send'*

If you find yourself writing in anger, save it and go for a cup of tea or coffee. When tempted to reply when upset or angry, always sleep on it and view your e-mail again with fresh eyes the next day. Imagine if tomorrow you saw your e-mail printed out and pinned up on the notice board.

Would you or your team members colleagues be surprised or ashamed by the tone or content? Hopefully they'd be pleased you had not lost your temper or risen to the bait when the sender had made a personal attack. They would respect the way you had calmly defended your point of view or were brave enough to admit your mistake if you were wrong.

Do consider your future relationship with the sender someone, with whom you may have to work in the months ahead. Don't leave a legacy of ill will that can come back to haunt you in the future.

6 *E-mail is neither secure nor private*
Don't send anything by e-mail that you wouldn't want posted
outside your door with your name attached. E-mail is not
secure. Your e-mails can be hacked by a malicious or merely
curious wrongdoer. If you receive an e-mail warning you
about a new virus, do not automatically forward it to your
entire address book as in all likelihood it will be a hoax. A
better course of action is to type the name of the virus into
Google. The search will usually reveal whether or not it is a
false alarm.

Many people believe that they have a right to privacy and are
not aware that if they work for a company, the e-mail system is
not a private mail system for the employees but rather it is the
property of the company to read and delete as it wishes. Indeed,
in many companies, the e-mail administrator has the right to
read any outgoing or incoming e-mails with consequences for
those who abuse the system with inappropriate mail.

7 *Respond promptly*
Try to acknowledge your relevant e-mails within a reasonable
time period – if not the same day then the following one. If you
cannot give a full reply immediately it is still courteous to send
a holding note which says something like: 'Thanks for your
e-mail. I can't deal with it now but I will get back to you first
thing tomorrow.' This does not leave the sender in the dark but
lets them know their e-mail has been received and when they can
expect a reply.

Senders who ask specific rather than general questions are likely
to get a quicker response.

8 *Show courtesy and respect*
Be careful not to click on 'Reply to all' when you meant to
click on 'Reply'. If your message is of a private or a personal
nature that you didn't intend to share with a wider audience,
the damage may be considerable. As a matter of courtesy ask
the sender's permission before forwarding a personal message.
It's all a matter of context. So if you receive an e-mail asking for
your help, it's fine to forward it to someone who can assist. On
the other hand forwarding an e-mail to make fun of someone is
clearly not acceptable.

When sending e-mail to a large group of recipients, don't use carbon copy (cc) as this will display the e-mail addresses of the entire group and may compromise their privacy. Instead use bcc (blind carbon copy) which will hide all the addresses and protect privacy. Using cc can also make the header part of the e-mail extremely long especially where there are a very large number of addresses. Type your own name into the cc space if you need to fill it.

9 *Style matters*
▶ Use simple English
Don't be too formal or use jargon unless you're sure the recipient will understand it. Use your own voice just as you would speak. Be natural. Don't try to be someone you aren't.

▶ Fonts
There is nothing worse than opening an e-mail and becoming blinded by the brightness elicited by all the words displaying in bold. It makes you want to instantly close the e-mail for the sake of protecting your eyes.

Additionally, fonts that are too small, too large, or otherwise hard to read (i.e. 8 point, times roman font, all bold) makes people not want to read the e-mail either.

Beware of your fonts in your 'presentation'. Do not bold the entire e-mail, use easy to read fonts such as Arial and use a standard size. Avoid lurid colours since they don't work well on all screens and can be hard to read. Also they won't be displayed at all if the reader has only plain text rather than HTML.

▶ Formatting
Make e-mails easy to read and quick to scan by using bullet points, numbered lists and keeping paragraphs short. Highlight keywords (bold or italic) for emphasis, without overdoing it.

▶ Minimize questions
Ask questions that matter and limit the number of questions and favours you ask in an e-mail (one or two at most). The more questions (especially open-ended ones) asked in one sitting, the less likely you are to get a response and the less likely all your questions will be answered.

Also, ask specific questions instead of a general open-ended one. Be reasonable and thoughtful when asking. Don't expect the recipient to solve all your life problems. Break them down into specifics and ask the one question that really matters.

You can send additional questions in separate e-mails. Don't overwhelm the receiver.

▶ Trimming of words
Like weeding a garden, read through the finished e-mail and trim out words, sentences, and paragraphs that do not contribute towards your desired result.

Check for potential ambiguities and unclear thinking. Can you rephrase sentences for clarity using fewer words? Check for excess commentary that doesn't add to the e-mail's main point. Remove extra details disclosed, unnecessarily.

▶ Check for sense and spelling
Spelling and grammatical mistakes are unprofessional and create a bad impression. Take the time to make your e-mails look professional. Use a spell checker. It won't catch every mistake but should catch some typos. When sending an e-mail that's really important it's a good idea to get a team member to check it for sense and accuracy before you hit 'Send'.

Never use all-caps capitalization as this denotes shouting.

Insight

Imagine you're writing your e-mail as a text message on a mobile phone, smart phone or blackberry. Without the luxury of a computer keyboard, your message will be much shorter. Do the same when you are at the computer and you'll keep your e-mails short and to the point.

10 *Make it easy to be found*
As part of your signature, include relevant URL addresses for your website, blog or any other locations. Make sure the links are active so the reader can reach them with a single click.

Sometimes e-mail is too fast!

A colleague once asked me for help and then almost immediately sent a follow-up informing me she had solved the problem on her own. But before reading her second message, I replied at length to the first. Once I learned that there was no need for any reply, I worried that my response would seem pompous, so I followed up with a quick apology: 'Should have paid closer attention to my e-mail.'

What I meant to say was '[I] should have looked more carefully at my [list of incoming] e-mail [before replying],' but I could tell from my colleague's terse reply that she had interpreted it as if I was criticizing her. If I hadn't responded so quickly to the first message, I would have saved myself the time I spent writing a long answer to an obsolete question. If I hadn't responded so quickly to the second message, I might not have alienated the person I had been so eager to help.

Dennis G. Jerz, Jerz's Literacy Weblog

Exercise
▶ Are your e-mails always to the point, short and simple?
▶ Do you ever click on 'Reply to all' when you meant to click on 'Reply'?
▶ Do you always think before you click 'Send'?

Think about the e-mails that you send. How could you make life easier for the receiver to read and understand them?

How to use one-on-one communication

Some team members find it hard to speak up in meetings. Sometimes it can be helpful to talk to them one-on-one. In fact one-on-one communication can serve a number of different purposes. As well as solving problems, it can be an opportunity for people to express their concerns in a way they could not do in a meeting. A one-on-one session should take place on their territory, not on yours. Ask them to suggest somewhere to meet where they feel comfortable.

BUILD TRUST
What if you can't get the team member to speak up? Don't make them feel uncomfortable but keep talking; over time you will build up the trust needed for them to feel confident enough to confide in you.

Ask at the end of the session if they have anything else of their mind. When they open up and say they do, make sure you listen!

BE A GOOD LISTENER

Always pay attention to your team members and listen to what they say rather than to what is going on inside your own head. Remember that you do not have all the answers and they usually know the job they do better than anyone else.

MAKE TIME FOR INDIVIDUAL TEAM MEMBERS

Regular one-on-one meetings with your team members are important. Show your team members that they have your full attention with no distractions, i.e. take the time to discuss their concerns and nothing else.

COMMUNICATE A CONSISTENT MESSAGE ABOUT YOUR VALUES

Your team members can make better decisions on their own when they know who you are and what you stand for. At all costs avoid sending mixed messages which will only confuse them.

GIVE REGULAR FEEDBACK

Keep the team in the loop. Don't let them be the last to learn about important company developments. Be in touch all the time and not just when there is a problem. Because team members are closest to the action, they can be valuable problem solvers and will often fix these on their own, providing you build up their confidence.

ACTING ON TEAM MEMBER FEEDBACK

Everyone needs to know how to handle criticism. You need to listen to what the team members have to say, ask questions where appropriate, get the team member's suggestions on how you could improve and then promise to consider it.

You may not agree with everything they say but listen and take it all in. Your immediate reaction might be to reject the feedback completely. This is not a good move since the team member who raised the comment will be discouraged from discussing issues in the future. Tell that team member that you need to take some time to think about the concern and get back to them later.

After you've given the issue some thought, you may still disagree. But do not ignore this person. Go back to them, acknowledge the fact that you both differ and say that it will not stand in the way of you working together positively. Promise to do all you can to build a strong relationship with them.

QUESTIONING SKILLS AND TECHNIQUES

Questioning techniques are very useful in one-on-one communication. They help prevent or reduce misunderstandings. They show you demonstrating genuine interest in the other person and also encourage team members to talk to you.

Exercise
▶ How often do you take the time to discuss your team members' concerns?
▶ How do you ensure you give them your full attention with no distractions, e.g. taking phone calls?
▶ How confident are you about handling criticism – from both sides?
▶ How do you make sure your team members know who you are and what you stand for?

KEYS TO A WINNING TEAM

What's the best way to communicate?

- Be aware of the range of communication tools available and use the most appropriate.

- Consider the right time and setting to call a meeting or send an e-mail or have a one-on-one session.

How to hold successful meetings:

- Hold meetings regularly for consistency.

- Vary the frequency with the type and nature of the business.

When running your meetings:

- use different questioning techniques, e.g. open, overhead, direct, redirect, relay.

How to write effective e-mails:

- Focus on the desired outcome and get to the point quickly.

- Keep it short, keep it simple and be yourself.

- Show courtesy and respect.

- Mistakes create a bad impression so always check your grammar; check your spelling.

How to use one-on-one communication:

- Find out what individual team members are thinking and win their confidence so they'll confide in you over time.

- Build trust and be a good listener.

- Make time for team members and show them they have your full attention.

- Give regular feedback and act on feedback from team members.

How to create a winning team

In this chapter you will learn:
- *how to face the challenges that come with being a team leader*
- *how to complete team assessments*
- *how to create a winning team!*

From the RAF Officer:

Can you be a good team leader without being confident, positive and focused?

> *I find this question particularly interesting because one instinctively thinks that this must be so. It depends on what you mean by confident. In dire circumstances when failure looks inevitable, a team leader would have to be stupid to be confident of the outcome. However, he has to have the confidence to make the best decisions in the circumstances to minimize the chances of failure. I can't help but think of Winston Churchill in this context.*

Any tips on team leading?

> *Making work fun usually helps. Lead by personality and don't expect people to do things that you are not prepared to do yourself. Everyone makes mistakes. Don't be hard on team members who make honest mistakes, where there was no stupid risk taking and nobody could have foretold the outcome.*

Anything further you want to add?

> *There is no definitive way to be a team leader. Each leader is different and has different skills. The style of leadership derives from the team itself, in terms of skills, strengths and weaknesses. The same leader would (and should) alter his style to suit the team needs.*

What have you done?

By now you have had the opportunity to acquire advice and information that will help you to:

- understand what teams do
- become a successful team leader
- create a balanced team
- work as a team
- make your team succeed
- improve your teamwork skills
- develop your team and yourself
- find the right way to talk to your team
- create a winning team.

Each step is one part of a journey towards becoming a great team leader. In conclusion, you can find here the key themes from the previous chapters and benefit from some final words of advice:

- Work as a team for a common purpose to achieve more than working alone.
- Adopt a style of leadership that builds trust and respect through listening and good communication.
- Find out the profiles of your team members so you can create a balanced team by assigning them an appropriate role.
- Be aware that teams develop over time, know which stage your team is at and understand what your team is for.
- Set SMART objectives, motivate the team and recognize great performers to help your team achieve results.
- Develop your skills for listening, communicating, building trust and planning so you will be trusted, confident, positive and focused.
- Consider team-building activities or events to develop your team and yourself so you can maximize the team's potential.
- Make sensible use of your team's time by communicating in the most appropriate manner through meetings, e-mails and one-on-one communication.
- Always remember that as a team leader you can make a difference and create a winning team!

From the RAF Officer:

As a team leader, can you make a real difference to your team and organization?

Almost certainly. It would take an extraordinary group of people to work symbiotically without some sort of leader. Even in such a group, a natural leader would emerge and take control.

Facing up to the challenges – solutions

Chapter 1 suggested that becoming a team leader can create ambivalent feelings in people. The examples were:

1 Your self-esteem is raised – but some colleagues may resent you for having been given this role.
2 You find yourself in the position of leading a team of people who just last week were your colleagues.
3 You enjoy the increased responsibility – but the pressures on your time are even greater.
4 You want to earn respect – but some of your team members are more senior to you.

Considering how these situations can be resolved, you will be pleased to know how you already possess many of the qualities needed to handle these areas of potential conflict. For those who find yourselves in these sorts of situations, *Create a Winning Team* can give you the confidence and the guidance to overcome them or resolve them. Let's revisit each challenge in turn.

1 *Your self-esteem is raised – but some colleagues may resent you for having been given this role.*

This is an issue of trust. See Chapter 7 for more information on building trust.

In his article titled '*Help! I got promoted and my colleagues resent me*' (CBS moneywatch.com) Ron Brown believes you need to recognize that promotions in this current economic climate are going to breed more resentment than ever, given the limited opportunities for advancement.

His advice is first to try to sort out which people resent you for simple, personal reasons of jealousy and those who are giving you the cold shoulder because they're more concerned about the impact of your new position on their career.

For the first type, those that are just jealous, Brown recommends that you need to accept the reality that some of your work relationships will be lost or at least changed and that this inevitably happens when you move on. You may regain some of these relationships later, but this won't come about by simply being nice to them. Your best bet to win them over is simply to be successful so that they're compelled to listen to you and respect you. So your strategy should be to be open and responsive to your colleagues but also as focused as possible on results.

For the second type, those that seem to be wary of you because of territorial issues, you need to work out how your new role affects the existing power and responsibilities of others.

Brown says to remember that your new position will likely have changed the landscape for others' opportunities for advancement. So these team members will be intent to maintain their own claims and will seek to resist your influence. As a result, you'll need to put up your guard against them and discuss with your allies in the organization how they can help you neutralize and overcome these people.

Finally he believes that, in general, your best response is to be clear with others about your new role and to make sure your manager communicates that to your peers and to other power players in your organization. Particularly when a move upsets the standard organizational structure like yours, it's vital to have clear signals from your bosses about your responsibilities and powers. And then just make sure you do the best job you can and see how your relationships with different people evolve.

Ron Brown, *Help! I got promoted and my colleagues resent me*, 18-8-2010, CBS
Moneywatch.com

The message is that you should accept the fact your promotion may cause resentment. The way to overcome this is to perform as a successful team leader, being open with your colleagues while being focused on results. Make sure, too, that your boss communicates your new role to your team members.

2 *You find yourself in the position of leading a team of people who just last week were your colleagues.*

This is an issue of leadership (see Chapter 3). The type of modern leadership that says it's what you do, not what you say is very relevant here.

Team members usually keep a close eye on their team leaders as role models to learn what is important to them at work. For example, the team leader who regularly arrives late is telling the team that punctuality doesn't matter.

As a team leader, you must set a positive example through your behaviour and attitude so your team members have a clear perception of how they are expected to conduct themselves. Your actions will speak louder than your words.

Think about the attitudes and behaviours you want your team members to demonstrate and practise. How have you shown these in your own conduct towards both customers and team members? If you haven't, you will probably need to reconsider your approach.

Let your team members see that the behaviours and attitudes you espouse are important. You're bound to make mistakes and fall short of your ideals from time to time. But you can expect to find that people are very forgiving provided they can see that you value them and that you believe in the high standards the team is being set. When you are tuned in to what's important to your team members and how they behave, you can greatly improve your team's performance.

When you're a new team leader you need to:

- ▶ respect your team's rules – both formal and informal
- ▶ learn as much as possible about your new team before trying to change it
- ▶ show in your own behaviour and attitudes those you wish to see in your team members
- ▶ be realistic about your own strengths and weaknesses
- ▶ understand what you do well and not so well.

The message here is to listen first before acting and then to lead by example. Following the above advice will help you gain the respect of those who were only recently your colleagues.

3 *You enjoy the increased responsibility – but the pressures on your time are even greater.*

As a matter of some urgency, you need to learn to handle the pressures on your time. If you don't, you may find the pressures build to a point where you get ill and cannot do your job. You may even get to the point where you have to resign your post because you can't handle the responsibilities in the time available.

Before you reach this point, there are a number of practical steps you can take to deal with this potentially harmful situation:

Be clear on responsibilities
First of all you should know – or establish – exactly what is expected from you. You may find you are being asked to take on a responsibility of which you were unaware.

Organize
Get organized so you know just what to do when. With more responsibility to handle, you need to have everything ready so you can act as soon as you need. At the start and end of each week, check that you are clear on what you should be doing. Be very clear on your objectives. When you are organized, you should be able to give your full attention to a single task so you won't end up sitting in front of your computer daydreaming because you haven't prioritized which task to tackle next.

Rest
Extra responsibility can lead to added stress unless you know how to handle it. The simple answer is rest. Leave the job behind when you leave the office for the night. Give your body a chance to recharge its batteries so you're ready for the next day's hassles. Only worry about the things you can change and then do something about them! Don't worry about things you cannot change. This sounds simple but it can take a long time to learn. Don't be put off at the prospect of increased responsibility. It's your opportunity to demonstrate what you are capable of. By avoiding the harmful effects of too much pressure, you will be able to enjoy it.

4 *You want to earn respect – but some of your team members are more senior to you.*

Show the right attitude and identify the personalities of your team members so that you can lead more effectively.

When working with more senior team members, one approach is to find a mentor with plenty of experience. Rooney Russell of Praendex Inc. advises 'Find out how they solved people problems in the past and partner with them.'

It takes time to build working relationships, but all too often time is in short supply in today's work place. To speed up this process it helps to be able to predict how your team members are likely to behave. Chapter 4 'Create a balanced team' deals in depth with this subject.

This understanding is critical in three major areas:

▶ how you communicate with each team member
▶ how you delegate responsibility to each team member
▶ how you facilitate decision-making within the team.

Strong communication is necessary

If you want your staff to ... buy into your vision, you need to adapt your communication style to the personalities of each person reporting to you.

Rooney Russell

You can do this using one of the personality profiling tools described in Chapter 4. These measure the behaviour and motivation of the team. The tools can help you see how their communication style differs from yours. They can very quickly help you understand your team's personality profiles and show you how these will affect business results.

For instance, if you are a team leader who is fast talking, fast thinking and a risk taker, then you need to be aware if other team members are more risk-averse. When talking to them, you will need to speak to their more cautious natures.

If a young team leader who is looking for quick results is supervising team members who are risk-averse, there's likely to be conflict. According to Russell, risk-averse people:

- ▶ need a great deal of data to make a decision
- ▶ hate to be wrong
- ▶ can't stand to be blamed if something goes amiss.

It often takes this type of personality a long time to make a decision.

To prevent such personalities from avoiding or delaying decisions, you must give them enough information to bolster their confidence in the decisions they're being asked to make.

> *You've also got to realize that some decisions are going to take longer than others and browbeating these people is not going to get the decision made any faster.*
>
> Rooney Russell

Russell also recommends that young team leaders should take great pains to assure their team that they will take ultimate responsibility for the team's decisions.

Delegate responsibility

When assigning tasks, you need to know if the task matches the strengths of the individual member of the team. Before delegating the details to a team member, you need to know, for example, whether the team member is someone who thrives on detail and can spend long hours focusing on the minutiae with the thoroughness required.

Alternatively, say you're a controlling type of personality – someone who wants things done just so – if you delegate a project to someone with a more easy going attitude, then problems are likely to arise. If things went wrong, the trust between you and your team member might be damaged for good.

Bridging the generation gap

Robert Norton, founder of StrategIT, an IT infrastructure consultancy, says:

> *Younger team leaders need to be aware of the age based cultural differences and speak to them.*

He says the 'work hard, play hard' crowd sometimes doesn't understand why everybody who works for them doesn't exhibit the same high energy and excitement about their careers and future. The willingness to stay extremely late to solve a particular problem is sometimes tempered by the age of the team member.

> *Whether it's because they have a family life with children at home or they're simply tired of working 70 or 80 hours a week, maintaining enthusiasm as you become more seasoned gets harder.*

Robert Norton

From his observations, young people often believe they have to put in the long hours to be successful.

For young team leaders, it does take time and hard work to win the respect of more senior team members but success can be yours by identifying the types of personalities you are working with and communicating openly and with respect from your side.

The lesson here is to respect the differences in the team and make reasonable allowances for the preferences and varying patterns of behaviour where your team is made up of people of a different age or gender. Revisit Chapter 4 'Create a balanced team' for advice on better understanding your team's personalities.

Insight

In terms of leading a team of former colleagues, or those of a different age group or a different gender, the first step is clearly to build trust and earn respect. As you have learned, this is achieved through open and honest communication and, above all, active listening.

Benefits of becoming a team leader

For all these challenges, becoming an excellent team leader brings additional responsibilities which require time to be done well. Being a team leader does, however, bring its own benefits by:

- creating personal job satisfaction
- allowing you to have a personal impact on the success of your section or department
- offering you the opportunity to improve your professional skills

- ▶ letting you participate in the future development of your company
- ▶ raising your profile with your manager and other senior personnel.

Insight

We could all take a lesson from the great northern geese which fly thousands of miles in perfect formation. Formation flying is 70 per cent more efficient than flying alone.

Dan Zandra

'How well do you work as a team?' assessment

Now try the assessment! It is really more of an activity you can do with your team as an exercise to identify strengths and weaknesses and to assess how well the team is currently performing. Each team member answers the questions individually, but the scores can be collated at the end to give a team total. There are 60 questions and the activity takes about an hour to complete.

The purpose of the assessment is to provide a way of finding out how well team leaders and members think the team is working at present.

You will need one copy of the Survey Sheet and the Diagnostic Sheet for each team member. Allow up to an hour for completion and discussion.

This is a useful diagnostic activity which enables all team members to contribute their opinions. It is scored to show the strengths and weaknesses of the team. The instructions are as follows:

1 Working as an individual, mark with a cross those statements which you feel apply to you or your team.
2 When you have worked through the 60 statements on the sheet, look at the Diagnostic Sheet.
3 Place a cross over those numbers on the Diagnostic Sheet which have been crossed on the Survey Sheet.
4 Add up the number of crosses in each column.

If you do it as a team, it's a good idea to collate and display the column totals for each member of the team. This gives you an overall view of the issues where the majority of the team requires most development. Use the interpretation information to help you decide which areas are most important to work on.

'HOW WELL DO YOU WORK AS A TEAM?'
ASSESSMENT – SURVEY SHEET

Put a cross against those statements with which you agree.

☐ I'm not comfortable with the way our team is managed or led.

☐ Our team seems to be detached from the rest of the department.

☐ I don't understand the significance of some things which happened in the past and to which other people keep referring.

☐ We disagree with each other about some fundamental issues.

☐ Our team is not very effective in its work.

☐ No one explains why you have to keep providing information to managers.

☐ It's not clear who takes which decisions in our team.

☐ Conflicts and rivalries between people inhibit our team.

☐ In our team, people just get on with their work. There's little social interaction.

☐ We often make plans but they never get followed through.

☐ There doesn't seem to be any consistent leadership for the team.

☐ I'm not clear what the overall purpose of our team is.

☐ We don't seem to learn from the past in defining our future.

☐ It would be difficult to say clearly what you stood for.

☐ People tend not to share their knowledge and skills with each other.

☐ Team meetings don't seem to work.

☐ I feel I'm not involved enough in decisions which affect my work.

☐ There isn't much support around for me.

☐ Whenever we reorganize or change, we seem to lose some of the important things that kept us together as a team.

☐ There are few opportunities for development and new learning.

☐ I am sometimes confused about whether I'm being told to do something or asked for my opinions about it.

☐ There seem to be lots of other teams and organizations doing similar work to us.

☐ We're not agreed on the direction for our work.

☐ People tend not to talk about their personal beliefs and opinions about the work.

☐ We keep meeting problems we don't know how to handle.

☐ I keep discovering that I've not been told things which are important to my work.

☐ We get consulted but nobody takes any notice of what we say.

☐ We don't get any positive feedback.

☐ It's not clear who's in our team.

☐ Our team just seems to be stuck.

☐ I often don't get appropriate feedback and support from my manager.

☐ We all seem to be working at different things.

☐ I don't know how our team got to be doing what it is now doing.

☐ I don't know what my colleagues think about work-related issues.

☐ My abilities are under used in this team.

☐ We don't have an effective system for sharing information.

☐ Everything is given to us as an instruction.

☐ People tend to work in isolation in this team without much communication with each other.

☐ People seem to have quite fixed roles; it's like they've been stereotyped.

☐ I feel that I'm not learning anything new.

☐ No one seems to be taking responsibility for organizing and maintaining our team.

- [ ] No one seems to value the work we do.

- [ ] All our work seems to be in bits and pieces; there's no coherent theme to it.

- [ ] We have no statement of our practice principles.

- [ ] Service users tend to complain a great deal about our work.

- [ ] We're swamped by paper that no one has time to read.

- [ ] Decisions seem to be taken at the wrong level.

- [ ] Lack of trust is an issue within the team.

- [ ] Our team doesn't seem to have any real identity of its own.

- [ ] We rarely stop and review what we're doing.

- [ ] It would be helpful if someone was championing the interests of our team to people outside.

- [ ] We always seem to focus on the detail without considering the whole picture.

- [ ] Members of our team seem to have different ideas about where we should be going.

- [ ] I don't agree with the way some of my colleagues are working.

- [ ] Sometimes I struggle to know how to do my job.

- [ ] Our team meetings are very predictable.

- [ ] No one thinks through the consequences of decisions.

- [ ] We don't often talk about how we're feeling.

- [ ] I don't know what happened to our team's history.

- [ ] We don't build any commitment to make change happen.

'HOW WELL DO YOU WORK AS A TEAM?' ASSESSMENT – DIAGNOSTIC SHEET

Transfer your crosses from the Survey Sheet to the box in the grid with the same number. Then add up the number of crosses in each column.

Leadership	Purpose	Direction	Values	Skills	Commun- ications	Decision- making	Support	Rites	Development
1	2	3	4	5	6	7	8	9	10
11	12	13	14	15	16	17	18	19	20
21	22	23	24	25	26	27	28	29	30
31	32	33	34	35	36	37	38	39	40
41	42	43	44	45	46	47	48	49	50
51	52	53	54	55	56	57	58	59	60

If you score three or more in any column, this suggests an area of team functioning which you feel would benefit from improvement. Consult the table below for a diagnosis.

Leadership	Aspects of the way in which the team is led or managed require attention.
Purpose	The overall purpose or goals of the team are unclear.
Direction	The past and future direction of the team's work require clarification.
Values	The team lacks agreement on shared values and principles in its work.
Skills	There may be a mismatch between the skills and knowledge required by the team and those currently possessed by team members.
Communica- tions	The way in which team members communicate with each other and share information might be improved.
Decision- making	Who takes responsibility for what decision is unclear.
Support	Team members are looking for improvements in the way they give or receive support in their work.
Rites	The social customs and rituals of the team require attention.
Development	Plans to review and develop the team into the future should be made.

Collate the column totals from other team members to give a team total.

Acknowledgements to Tim Pickles (www.timpickles.com) as author and copyright holder. Assessment was originally published on TrainingZone (www.trainingzone.co.uk)

You can create your own winning team

At the start this book promised to be down to earth, practical, with a no nonsense approach. A team leader has been described as one who guides and inspires others. In the end, you need just six key words to create a winning team:

- ▶ trust
- ▶ respect
- ▶ leadership
- ▶ communication
- ▶ listening
- ▶ planning.

Build trust
Above all there has to be trust between team leader and team members. Without trust the team cannot work collaboratively. Activity breaks down.

Earn respect
As a team leader, particularly as a new team leader, you need to earn the respect of the other team members in order to be an effective leader.

Lead from the front and value your followers
Leadership is at the heart of teamwork but there can be no leadership without followers.

Listen hard and communicate fully
Communication is two-way – receiving and transmitting. Listening is more important than talking.

Prepare to plan
When you can plan and project manage, you have the capacity to look ahead and remove the obstacles that block your team's path.

By faithfully embracing, absorbing and then practising these six simple actions, you can be confident that you can create your own winning team.

Postscript: a letter from the author to team leaders

Dear team leader,

As a parting gesture, I want to pass on to you some key points that have impressed me while writing this book. I hope they will be useful and relevant to your role as team leader.

When you become a team leader for the first time, it is both a challenge and an opportunity but it can also be daunting to be leading former colleagues and more senior team members. So the first thing you must do is build the team on what we have called emotional strength.

This means gaining the team's trust through being open, honest, fair and, above all, keeping your promises. If they don't believe what you say, they won't perform well for you. Some team leaders fail because they believe that knowledge equals power and that they can control the team by withholding information from them. In fact, the opposite is true.

By communicating openly and honestly, you keep the team in the loop, for example, by making sure they learn promptly about important company developments. Keep in touch all the time, not just when there's a problem. In this way you will also earn your team's respect. Build your team on trust.

Next be very clear about what you are taking on and where your role starts and ends. Have clear SMART objectives for the tasks and projects you undertake and focus on the outcomes with measures to show when you have achieved them.

In setting these objectives, consult and seek feedback from the team even where people disagree with you. Learn to handle criticism by listening to what the team members have to say, asking questions where appropriate and getting team members' suggestions on how you could improve. The days are fortunately in the past when the leader issued commands and they were obeyed without question. That old-fashioned style stifles initiative and innovation. Rather, lead from the front by setting an example through your own behaviour and attitudes. Let people judge you by what you do.

While adopting a democratic approach, remember that you are always the team leader and that you must not be afraid to take decisions, however tough. Organizations often fail because their managers lack the will to lead and avoid difficult issues. At the same time don't be afraid of making mistakes. Once you have the team's trust, they will be very forgiving. Likewise cultivate a culture where the team knows you will be tolerant, without being uncritical, when they slip up in their turn.

In learning how to relate to the team individually, the message from the personality models is that everyone is different and responds in different ways. Your task is to work out what types of people you have in your team and then learn to adapt your behaviour to match theirs. It's a dynamic relationship where you should take the lead. This will make your life much less stressful as it will avoid unnecessary conflict.

Finally, think about succession planning and the time in the future when you may want to progress your own career and move up in the organization. If you don't develop and train a suitable candidate from within the team to take your place, your managers may feel you are irreplaceable!

Good luck with creating a winning team!

Kevin Benfield

Taking it further

Now that you have read *Create a Winning Team*, you may wish to explore the subject further. Below you will find a list of books and references listed by chapter. These were helpful in the writing of the book and will help you develop your team leadership knowledge and skills in more depth.

Chapter 2:

Covey, Stephen, M.R., *The Speed of Trust* (Simon & Schuster, 2006).

Kotter, John P., *Leading Change* (Harvard Business School Press, 1996).

Woodcock, Mike and Francis, Dave, *Teambuilding Strategy*, (Gower Publishing Ltd, 1994)

Chapter 3:

Ackoff & Addison, *A Little Book Of F-Laws – 13 Common Sins Of Management* (Triarchy Press, 2006).

Adair, John, *Effective Leadership: How to be a successful leader* (Pan, 2009).

Adair, John, *Develop Your Leadership Skills* (Kogan Page, 2007).

Gratton, Lynda, *Glow. How You Can Radiate Energy, Innovation and Success* (FT Prentice Hall, Pearson Education, 2009).

Hersey, Paul and Blanchard, Ken, *Management of Organizational Behaviour* (Pearson Education, 2007).

Kotter, John P., *Leader to Leader* (Drucker Foundation and Jossey-Bass Inc., 1998).

Pardey, David, Introducing Leadership (Butterworth-Heinemann, 2006).

Selden, Bob, *What To Do When You Become The Boss* (Business Plus, 2010).

Udwin, Mike, *Management doesn't work until your teams well led* (Free report from: http://managementdoesntwork.weebly.com/details-page-cd-and-report.html).

Chapter 4:

Belbin, Dr R. M., *Management Teams–Why They Succeed Or Fail* (Butterworth-Heinemann, 2010).

Dellinger, Dr Susan, *Communicating Beyond Our Differences: Introducing the Psycho-Geometrics™ System* (Prentice-Hall/Jade Ink, 1989 & 1996).

Porter, Elias H., *Strength Deployment Inventory*® (Pacific Palisades, CA: Personal Strengths Assessment Service, 1971).

Chapter 5:

Citrin, James and Neff, Thomas, *You're in Charge, Now What?* (Three Rivers Press, CA, 2007).

de Bono, Edward, *Six Thinking Hats* (Viking, 1986).

Charrier, George O., *Cog's Ladder: A Model of Group Growth* (Procter and Gamble company newsletter, 1972).

Tuckman, Bruce, *Forming – Storming – Norming – Performing model of group development* (1965).

Tuckman, Bruce, *Developmental Sequence in Small Groups* (Psychological Bulletin 63 pp384-399, 1965).

Chapter 6:

Grote, Dick, *Discipline without punishment* (Amacom, 2006).

Chapter 7:

Epstein, Robert, *The Big Book of Creativity Games: Quick, Fun Activities for Jumpstarting Innovation* (McGraw Hill, 1995).

Johnson, Kerry L., *Selling with NLP* (Nicholas Brealey Publishing, 1994).

Chapter 8:

Hadfield-Law, Lisa, *Train You Team Yourself! How To Design and Deliver Effective In-House Training Courses* (How To Books Ltd, 2002).

Lencioni, Patrick, *The Five Dysfunctions of a Team: A Leadership Fable*, (Jossey-Bass, 2002).

Chapter 10:

Pickles, Tim, *Toolkit for Trainers* (Pavilion Publishing, 1999).

Additional information:

There is also a wealth of useful information on team leadership on the internet. The links used for reference for this book are given as they occur.

For a source of team-building events see Progressive Resources www.teambuilding.co.uk

For training and development in team leadership including qualifications, see the Institute of Learning & Management www.i-l-m.com

Index

Image credits